WORDS OF COUN SEL

Register This New Book

Benefits of Registering*

- ✓ FREE **replacements** of lost or damaged books

- ✓ FREE **audiobook** – *Pilgrim's Progress,* audiobook edition

- ✓ FREE information about new titles and other **freebies**

WORDS OF COUN SEL

FOR ALL LEADERS, TEACHERS, AND EVANGELISTS

CHARLES H. SPURGEON

We love hearing from our readers. Please contact us at www.anekopress.com/questions-comments with any questions, comments, or suggestions.

Words of Counsel – Charles H. Spurgeon
Revised Edition Copyright © 2017

Cover Design: Jonathan Lewis
Editors: Sheila Wilkinson and Ruth Zetek

Aneko Press

www.anekopress.com

Aneko Press, Life Sentence Publishing, and our logos are trademarks of
Life Sentence Publishing, Inc.
203 E. Birch Street
P.O. Box 652
Abbotsford, WI 54405

RELIGION / Christian Life / Spiritual Growth

Paperback ISBN: 978-1-62245-502-7
eBook ISBN: 978-1-62245-503-4

10 9 8 7 6 5 4 3 2

Available where books are sold

Contents

Chapter 1

One Soul that Repents

A word fitly spoken is like apples of gold inscribed with silver. – Proverbs 25:11

Half a dozen words from a tender mother to a son as he leaves home for college or an apprenticeship may drop like gentle dew from heaven upon him. A few sentences from a kind and discreet father to an unconverted daughter, and kind and affectionate words to her husband as they enter married life may make that household a house of God forever. That father had taken the advice of the apostle Paul when he said, *Let your word be always with grace, seasoned with salt, that ye may know how ye ought to answer each one* (Colossians 4:6). A kind word dropped by a brother to a sister or a little letter written from a sister to her brother may be God's arrow of grace. Such little things as a tear or an anxious glance have the ability to work wonders.

You may have heard of Mr. Whitefield, who made

it his habit to talk to the members of the household about their souls wherever he stayed.[1] He spoke with each one personally, but when he stopped at a certain house with a colonel, he found this man to be and have everything he ever wanted, except he was not a Christian. Whitefield was so pleased with the hospitality and so charmed with the general character of the colonel and his wife and daughters that he did not want to speak to them about their lack of faith in Christ as he would have done with other individuals. He had stayed with them for a week, and during the last night, the Spirit of God spoke to his heart about this, such that he could not sleep.

"These people," he thought, "have been very kind to me, and I have not been faithful to them; I must do it before I go. I must tell them that whatever good thing they have, if they do not believe in Jesus, they are lost." He arose and prayed. After praying, he still felt contention in his spirit. His old nature said, "I cannot do it," but the Holy Spirit seemed to say, "Don't leave them without warning." At last, he thought of a way and prayed to God to accept it. He used his ring and wrote these words upon a diamond-shaped pane of glass in the window: "One thing you lack." He could not bring himself to speak to them but went his way with much prayer for their conversion.

No sooner had he left than the good woman of the house, who admired him very much, said, "I will go up

---

1   George Whitefield (1714-1770) was an Anglican priest and a powerful orator of the eighteenth century who defied church authority and preached outdoors. He is credited with igniting the Great Awakening in America.

to his room. I like to look at the very place where the man of God has been." She went up and noticed the windowpane with those words, "One thing you lack." It struck her with conviction in a moment. "Ah!" said she. "I thought he did not care much about us, for I knew he always pleaded with those with whom he stayed; when he did not do so with us, I thought we had annoyed him. But now I see he was too tender in mind to speak to us."

She called her daughters up. "Look there, girls," she said. "See what Mr. Whitefield has written on the window! 'One thing you lack.' Call up your father."

And the father came up and read, "One thing you lack." They all knelt around the bed where the man of God had slept, and asked God to give them the one thing they lacked. When they left that chamber, they had found that one thing, and the whole household rejoiced in Jesus.

Earnestness often produces discretion and helps man use tact if not talent.

Not long ago I met with a friend who knows the church member who preserves that very pane of glass in her family as an heirloom. Now, if you are not able to admonish and warn in one way, do it in another; take care to be blameless of your relatives and friends, that you may not be guilty before God. So live, speak, and teach by one means or another that you will have been faithful to God and faithful to the souls of men.

Earnestness often produces discretion and helps man use tact if not talent. The apostle Andrew used what ability he had. If he had been like some young men, he would have said, "I'd like to serve God. How I'd like to preach! And I'd attract a large congregation!" Well, there is a pulpit in every street, which is a wide, effectual door for preaching in our great city beneath God's blue sky. But some enthusiastic young men would prefer nicer accommodations than the open air. If they are not invited to the largest pulpits, they do nothing.

How much better it would be if they were like Andrew, and used the abilities they had among those who are accessible to them. *He* [Andrew] *first found his own brother Simon and said unto him, We have found the Messias, which is, being interpreted, the Christ. And he brought him* [Simon] *to Jesus* (John 1:41-42). From that first step came something else, and from that, something else, and so on year after year. Andrew had been the means of bringing his brother to Jesus. Christ had some reason in the choice of His apostles to their office, and perhaps the reason for His choice of Andrew was that he was an earnest man. He brought Simon Peter to Jesus.

Young men, if you are diligent in tract distribution and diligent in Sunday school, you are likely men who could be ministers. But if you stop and do nothing until you can do everything, you will remain useless – an impediment to the church instead of a help.

Dear sisters in Jesus Christ, you must never think that you can do nothing at all. God could never make such a mistake. You have talent entrusted to you – something given to you to enable you to do what no one else can do. Find out what it is and settle into it. Ask God to tell you what your niche is and stand in it, doing your work until Jesus Christ comes and gives you your reward. Use what ability you have, and use it at once.

Andrew proved his wisdom in that he focused on a single soul. He directed all his efforts toward one man. Afterwards, Andrew may have reached out to many more, but he began with one. One soul that repents sets all of heaven's bells ringing. *There is joy in the presence of the angels of God over one sinner that repents* (Luke 15:10).

What if you spend your whole life pleading and laboring for the conversion of that one child? If you win that pearl, it shall be worth your life of labor. Don't be discouraged if your class decreases in numbers or if most of those you labor with reject your testimony.

If a man could earn only one in a day, he might be satisfied. "One what?" you ask. I did not mean one penny, but one thousand dollars. "Ah," you say, "that would be an immense reward." So if you earn but one soul, you must determine what that one is worth. In numbering, it is only one, but for value, it exceeds all that earth values. *For what shall it profit a man, if he shall gain the whole world and lose his soul?* (Mark 8:36). What loss would it be to you, if you lost all the world but gained your soul, when God made you useful for winning the souls of others? Be content and labor where you are, even if your work is small, and you will be wise.

You may imitate Andrew in not going far away to do mission work. Many Christians work diligently many miles from their own house, when they could stay where they are and spend that time in the vineyard at home. I do not think it would be wise to require a city in the eastern part of the country to remove snow in the Midwest, or a community in the West to harvest crops in the South. It is most efficient for each area to work in and care for their own communities and resources. Likewise, as believers we should do all the work we can in the place where God has been pleased to locate us – especially in our own households.

If every man has a claim upon me, my own offspring have more. If every woman has some demand upon me as to her soul, my own flesh and blood have more. My duty or responsibility, as well as charity, must begin at home. Conversion should begin with those who are nearest to us in ties of relationship. I urge you not to attempt foreign missions, not to pity those in Africa, and not to weep over heathen lands before your own children, your own flesh and blood, your own neighbors, and your own acquaintances. Lift your cry to heaven for them, and later you can preach among the nations. Andrew later went to Cappadocia, but he began with his brother Simon. You may labor wherever you please in years to come, but reach your own household and those who are under your guardianship first. Be wise in this thing: use the ability you have and use it among those who are near to you.

Perhaps somebody will ask, "How did Andrew persuade Simon Peter to come to Christ?"

He did so first by telling his own personal experience. He said, *We have found the Messias* (John 1:41). Tell others what you have experienced in Christ.

Next, Andrew explained to Simon what it was he

had found. He did not say he had found someone who had impressed him but didn't know who he was; he told him he had found the Messiah – the Christ. Be clear in your knowledge of the gospel and your experience of it; then tell the good news to those you desire to reach.

Then Andrew had power over Peter because of his own decided conviction. He did not say, "I hope I have found Christ," but "I have found him." He was sure of that. Grasp the full assurance of your own salvation – *ye were sealed with that Holy Spirit of the promise* (Ephesians 1:13). There is no weapon like it. He that speaks with doubt of what he tries to convince another asks that other person to doubt his testimony. Be positive in your experience and your assurance, for this will help you.

> He that speaks with doubt of what he tries to convince another asks that other person to doubt his testimony.

Andrew had power over Peter because he put the good news before him in an earnest fashion. He did not talk as though it were a commonplace fact and say, "The Messiah has come," but he communicated to him as though it was the most important of all messages. Probably with voice inflections and hand gestures, he exclaimed, *We have found the Messias, which is, . . . the Christ.* Tell your own family about your belief, your enjoyments, and your assurance. Tell everything sensibly with assurance of the truth, and who can tell whether God might bless your effort?

Andrew brought his brother to Jesus and what a treasure he was! Christ made him a soul fisherman. We know of no others who caught three thousand souls in a single haul with the first cast of the gospel net (Acts 2:41). Peter, a very prince in the Christian church, one of the mightiest of the servants of the Lord in all his usefulness, would be a comfort to Andrew. I wouldn't doubt that in his days of doubt and fear, Andrew might have said, "I am thankful that my dear brother Peter is honored in bringing souls to Christ."

You might still produce the music of a heart that until now has not been tuned to the praise of Christ. You are to kindle the fire, which shall light up a sacred sacrifice of a consecrated life to Christ. Most important: be up and doing for the Lord Jesus, be persistent and prayerful, be zealous and self-sacrificing. *Be ye doers of the word, and not hearers only, deceiving your own selves* (James 1:22). When we have validated our God by prayer, He will pour more blessings on us than we are able to hold.

Chapter 2

Angels in Sodom

That utterance may be given unto me, that I may open my mouth with confidence, to make known the mystery of the gospel, for which I am an ambassador in chains, that in this I may speak boldly as I ought to speak. – Ephesians 6:19-20

Every believer should be an ambassador from heaven. Jesus said to His disciples, *As my Father has sent me, even so send I you* (John 20:21). Later, the apostle Paul told the Corinthians, *Now then we are ambassadors for Christ, as though God did exhort you by us; we beseech you in Christ's name, be ye reconciled to God* (2 Corinthians 5:20). You are sent to gather – to seek and to save the Lord's lost sheep. I speak solemnly to you who are proving your true love to souls by your work for them, and I remind you that it is a glorious work to seek to save men, and for this reason you should be willing to endure the greatest possible inconveniences.

The angels never hesitated when they were told to go to Sodom. They descended without hesitating and went about their work, because the report of Sodom's detestable iniquity had gone up to heaven, and the Lord could not bear that filthy city any longer. From the purity of heaven, the angels beheld the infamy of Sodom. God sent them, and they did not fail to go.

And the two angels came to Sodom at evening (Genesis 19:1). What? Angels? Did angels come to Sodom? To Sodom, but still angels? Yes, and no less angelic because they came to Sodom, but even more so. With unquestioning obedience to their Master's command, they sought out Lot and his family to deliver them from impending destruction.

However near to Christ you may be, or however much your character may be like your Lord's, if you are called to such service, you must never refuse. You should never say, "I cannot talk to these people, they are so depraved and debased; I cannot enter that sinful hangout to tell them about Jesus.

If you are called to such service, you must never refuse.

I get sick at the thought; the revelers are too revolting for my comfort." Instead, because men of God are wanted there, you must be found there. Whom does the physician go to but the sick? And where best can the distributer of donations direct the gifts as among those who are spiritually destitute?

Be angels of mercy, and God may speed you in your

soul-saving work. As you have received Christ Jesus into your hearts, imitate Him in your lives. Let the woman who is a sinner receive your kindness, for Jesus looked on her with mercy. Let the man who has been mad with wickedness be sought after, for Jesus healed demoniacs. Let no type of sin, however terrible, be thought of as beneath your empathy or beyond your labor. But seek out those who have wandered the farthest and snatch them from the flame of the firebrands.

When you go to lost souls, you must tell them plainly of their condition and their danger as these angels did. They said, *Up, get you out of this place; for the LORD will destroy this city* (Genesis 19:14). If you long to save men's souls, you must tell them a great deal of disagreeable truth. The preaching of the wrath of God is sneered at today, and even good people are half-ashamed of it. A soppy sentimentality about love and goodness has hushed plain gospel teaching and warnings. But, if we expect souls to be saved, we must declare the terrors of the Lord without flinching but with all affectionate faithfulness.

"Well," said a young lad when he heard the minister tell his congregation that there was no hell, or at any rate only a temporary punishment, "I don't need to come and hear this man any longer. If it is as he says, everything is all right, and religion is of no consequence. If it is not as he says, then I must not listen to him again, because he will deceive me."

Even the apostle Paul wrote, *Therefore being certain of that terror of the Lord, we persuade men* (2 Corinthians 5:11). We shouldn't let modern squeamishness prevent plain speaking. Are we to be gentler than the apostles? Are we wiser than the inspired preachers of the Word? Until we are overcome with the dread thought of the sinner's doom, we are not fit for preaching to the unconverted. We will never persuade men if we are afraid to speak of the judgment and the condemnation of the unrighteous. No one is as infinitely gracious as our Lord Jesus Christ, yet no preacher has ever uttered more faithful words of thunder than He did. He spoke of the place *where their worm does not die, and the fire is never quenched* (Mark 9:44). It was He who said, *They shall go away into eternal punishment* (Matthew 25:46). He told the parable about the man in hell who longed for a drop of water to cool his tongue:

> *And it came to pass that the beggar died and was carried by the angels into Abraham's bosom; the rich man also died and was buried; and in Hades he lifted up his eyes, being in torments, and saw Abraham afar off and Lazarus in his bosom. And he cried and said, Father Abraham, have mercy on me and send Lazarus that he may dip the tip of his finger in water and cool my tongue; for I am tormented in this flame. But Abraham said, Son, remember that thou in thy lifetime didst receive thy good things, and likewise Lazarus evil things; but now he is comforted here, and thou art tormented.* (Luke 16:22-25)

We must be as plain as Christ was, as honest to the souls of men, or we may be called to account for our unfaithfulness in the end. If we flatter our friends with fond dreams of insignificant future punishment, they will eternally detest us for deluding them. They will invoke perpetual curses upon us for having prophesied smooth things but withholding the awful truth from them.

First, we must affectionately and plainly tell the sinner that the *wages of sin is death* and disaster will come from his unbelief (Romans 6:23). Then we must beg the guilty to escape from the deserved destruction. Though the angels understood that God had elected Lot to be saved, they did not omit a single warning or leave the work to itself, as though it were to be done by predestination apart from instrumentality.[2] They said to Lot, *Arise, take thy wife and thy two daughters who are here; lest thou be consumed* (Genesis 19:15). How impressive is each admonition! What force and eagerness of love we see with each plea! *Escape; for thy soul, do not look behind thee, neither stop thou in all the plain; escape to the mountain, lest thou be consumed* (Genesis 19:17). Every word is quick and powerful, decisive and to the point.

---

2   Lot was considered a righteous man. First, Abraham interceded for Lot: *And he* [Abraham] *said, Oh let not the Lord be angry, and I will speak yet but this once; peradventure ten* [righteous] *shall be found there. And he* [the Lord] *said, I will not destroy it for ten's sake* (Genesis 18:32). The apostle Peter also makes mention of Lot's righteousness: *And if he* [God] *condemned by destruction the cities of Sodom and Gomorrha, turning them into ashes, making them an example unto those that after should love without fear and reverence of God; and delivered just Lot, who was persecuted by those abominable people because of their nefarious conversation; (for that righteous man dwelling among them, in seeing and hearing, afflicted his righteous soul from day to day with the deeds of those unjust people); the Lord knows how to deliver the godly out of temptations and to reserve the unjust unto the day of judgment to be punished* (2 Peter 2:6-9).

13

Souls want earnest rebuke and affectionate encouragement to keep them from their own ruin. If they were wise, the simple information of their danger would be enough, and the prospect of a happy ending would be sufficient. But since they are not wise, they must be urged, persuaded, and begged to look to the crucified Christ that they may be saved. We would never have come to Christ without divine pressure upon us, and neither will they.

Since that pressure usually comes by some instrumentality or intermediary, let us seek to be such instruments. If it had not been for earnest voices that spoke to us and earnest teachers that beckoned us to come to the cross, we would not have come. Let us therefore repay the debt we owe to the church of God and seek to do for others what God in His mercy has done for us. Let us persuade men with all our powers of reasoning and argument, salting our words with tears of affection. Don't let any doctrinal issues stand in the way of persuading the minds of men, for sound doctrine is perfectly reconcilable later.

I remember complaints being made against a sermon of mine, titled "Compel them to come in," in which I spoke with much tenderness for souls. That sermon was said to be Arminian and unsound. To be judged by men is a small matter to me, for my Master set His seal on that message. I never preached a sermon where so many souls were won to God, as our church meetings can testify. All over the world where this sermon has been shared, sinners have been saved through its instrumentality. Therefore, if it is vile to instruct and encourage sinners, I purpose to be viler still.

I am as firm a believer in the doctrines of grace as any man living, and a true Calvinist after the order of John Calvin himself, but if it is an evil thing to bid the sinner to lay hold of eternal life, I will be yet more evil in this respect. Herein I imitate my Lord and His apostles. They taught that salvation is by grace and grace alone and spoke to men as rational beings and responsible agents. Jesus said to them, *Enter ye in at the narrow gate*, and *Labour not for the food which perishes, but for the food which abides unto eternal life* (Matthew 7:13; John 6:27). Cling to the great truth of divine sovereignty, but don't let it hinder you when, in the power of the Holy Spirit, you become fishers of men.

> Where words are not sufficient, as often happens, you must adopt other modes of persuasion.

Where words are not sufficient, as often happens, you must adopt other modes of persuasion. The angels took Lot and his family by the hand. I have much faith under God in close dealings with men; personal entreaties by the power of the Holy Spirit do wonders. To grasp a man's hand while you speak with him may be wise and helpful; sometimes if you can hold a person's hand and show your anxiety by pleading with him, God will bless your effort. When you cast your words quietly and solemnly, as men drop pebbles into a well, right into the depth of a man's soul when he is alone, you may

15

be more effectual than the preacher who has labored in vain with his sermon.

If you cannot win men by words, you must say to yourself, "What can I do?" Then go to the Lord with the same inquiry. With diligent conviction you must provoke them into thoughtfulness. As the woman exasperated the unjust judge, so you can tire the lost souls until they listen to you, if for no other reason than to be rid of you. If you cannot reach them because they will not read the Bible, maybe you can give them a good book which may say what you cannot say. You can write them a short, earnest letter and tell them how you feel. You can continue in prayer for them, stir up the arm of God, and beseech the Most High to come to the rescue.

Sometimes, when everything else has failed, a tear of disappointed love has done the work. One day when Mr. Knill was distributing tracts amongst the soldiers, he was met by a man who cursed him. This man told his fellow soldiers, "Make a ring round him, and I will stop his tract-distributing once and for all." Then he uttered such fearful oaths and curses that Mr. Knill burst into a flood of tears.

Years later when he was preaching in the streets, a soldier came up and said, "Mr. Knill, do you know me?"

"No, I do not," he said. "I don't know that I have ever seen you."

"Do you remember the soldier who said, 'Make a ring round him and stop his tract-distributing'? Do you recall what you did?"

"No, I do not."

"Why, you broke into tears, and when I got home, those tears melted my heart. I saw you were so sincere that I felt ashamed of myself, and now I preach that same Jesus whom I once despised."

Oh, that you might have such a strong love for perishing sinners that you will endure their rejections and rebukes and say to them, "Strike me if you will, but hear me. Ridicule me, but I will still plead with you. Cast me under your feet as though I were refuse, but I will not let you perish, if it is in my power to warn you of your danger."

We ought to remember that we are the messengers of God's mercy to the sons of men. *The LORD being merciful unto him; and they brought him forth and set him outside the city* (Genesis 19:16). The angels had not come to Lot on their own; they were the embodiment and outward display of God's mercy. Christians in the world should view themselves as manifestations of God's mercy, instruments of grace, and servants of the Holy Spirit.

> God can save men without instruments or intermediaries, but He very seldom does.

Now mercy is a nimble attribute. Justice lingers; it is shod with lead, but the feet of mercy are winged. Mercy delights to perform its duty. So we should delight in doing good to men. God can save men without instruments or intermediaries, but He very seldom does. His usual rule is to work by means of someone or something. If only the mercy of God would work mightily by us! Let's remember that as we mingle with society, God has committed the ministry of reconciliation to us. *God, who reconciled us to himself by Jesus Christ, and gave us the ministry of reconciliation; . . . and having placed in us the word of reconciliation* (2 Corinthians 5:18-19).

If angels had been sent to this earthly ministry, surely they would be continually active. They would fly with all their might from place to place to do the Lord's will. Shouldn't we, who are honored to have this ministry, be as active as they would be? As much as we are able, let us *walk circumspectly, not as fools, but as wise, redeeming the time, because the days are evil* (Ephesians 5:15-16). Let us *be instant in season and out of season*, and let us *sow upon all waters* (2 Timothy 4:2; Isaiah 32:20). Let it be our earnest endeavor to confirm our service, whatever that service may be, so it may be said, *Well done, thou good and faithful slave; thou hast been faithful over a few things; I will set thee over many things* (Matthew 25:21).

Chapter 3

Diligence in Christ

But thanks be to God, who gives us the
victory through our Lord Jesus Christ.
– 1 Corinthians 15:57

Someone might ask, "How is it that we can hope to make an impression upon the present age? What means do we have except the simple gospel of Jesus Christ?" We are certainly not wealthy, and we are not considered the great ones of the land. Our membership has always been among the poor. How shall we expect to share with a city or exert any influence upon such a great country? Above all, how shall we make any impression on the population of the whole globe?

We are weak, but we are not weaker than the first disciples of Christ. They were not educated; neither were they the wealthy of the earth. Most of them were fishermen with no cultivated ability. Wherever they went, they wielded the sword of the Spirit, which is the Word of God, and their enemies became confused. Some of them died in conflict; some were slain by the sword, and others were torn apart by wild beasts. But as Paul said, *in all these things we are more than conquerors through him that loved us* (Romans 8:37). The early church did tell its generation the good news and left a seed behind that the whole earth could not destroy. By God's grace we will do the same if we are equally determined, equally filled with the divine life, equally resolved by any means and by all means, to spread the affection of Jesus Christ. Our weakness shall be our strength, for God will make it the platform upon which the omnipotence of His grace shall be displayed. When Paul prayed to have the thorn removed from his flesh, the Lord told him, *My grace is sufficient for thee; for my strength is made perfect in weakness* (2 Corinthians 12:9).

> **May the King Himself lead us onward, and we shall not fear the result.**

Keep together; keep close to Christ, *for with the LORD there is mercy and plenteous redemption close to him* (Psalm 130:7). Heed the battle cry; hold fast the faith; *hold fast the profession of our hope without wavering (for he is faithful that promised)* (Hebrews 10:23). Quit yourselves like men in the conflict, and the gates of hell shall not prevail against you. May the King Himself lead us onward, and we shall not fear the result.

As the hart pants after the water brooks, so does my soul pant after thee, O God (Psalm 42:1). If we pant to see the Word of God increase and a great company of those who are least likely to be saved are brought in, an adequate intermediary or messenger must strive and labor for them. Nothing can succeed without the work of the Holy Spirit and the smile from heaven. Paul *planted, Apollos watered, and God gave the increase* (1 Corinthians 3:6). We must never list our outward means of evangelism without referring to that blessed and mysterious Power who abides in the church, without whom nothing is good, nothing is efficient, and nothing is successful.

> "Come, Holy Spirit, heavenly Dove,
> With all Thy quickening powers."[3]

This should be our first prayer whenever we attempt to serve God, for if we begin with pride, we can have little hope to succeed with all our efforts. If we plunge ahead without the Spirit, we shouldn't be surprised if we return with defeat. O Spirit of the living God, if it were not for Your power, we could not make the attempt; but when we rely upon You, we can go forward in confidence.

I have been struck by the remarkable honesty of the testimonies of the early preachers as I look through the history of the Reformation and the times before the Reformation. If you look at the life of Farel, you find him not preaching *about* the gospel, but preaching *the gospel.* John Calvin was the same. He is looked upon now as only a theologian, but he was really one of the greatest gospel preachers. When Calvin opened the

---

3   Isaac Watts, "Come, Holy Spirit, Heavenly Dove," 1707.

Book and took a text, you would be sure that he was about to preach *by grace are ye saved through faith and that not of yourselves: it is the gift of God* (Ephesians 2:8).

And it was the same with Luther. Luther's preaching was the ringing of a big bell, the note that always said, *Believe on the Lord Jesus Christ, and thou shalt be saved* (Acts 16:31)! It is *not of works, lest any man should boast*, but by faith are ye saved, and by faith alone (Ephesians 2:9). They preached this, and they preached it again; they did not bury the doctrine in difficult words, but they labored with all their might, so both the farmer at the plow and the fishwife in the market could comprehend the truth. They did not aim at lofty speeches and flowing eloquence; they had a most contemptible opinion of such rhetoric. They just plunged in with this one truth: *He that believes in the Son has eternal life*, and *Believe on the Lord Jesus Christ, and thou shalt be saved* (John 3:36; Acts 16:31). If we are to see the church of God restored to her original glory, we must have this plain, simple gospel preaching. I do believe that hiding the cross beneath the veil of fine language and educated dissertation is half the cause of the spiritual destitution of our country. Jesus Christ came into the world to save sinners, not to give an eloquent dissertation.

We must not only have plain preaching, but plain teaching also. Sunday school teachers must teach this same gospel. One denomination has confessed that after their schoolrooms were crowded with children, they did not know if any of those children attended at the places of worship later. What a miserable, sad admission!

And haven't we known teachers who believed in the doctrines of grace and fought earnestly for them, but in the schoolroom, they prattled to the little children in foolish chatter? They tell them, "Be good boys and girls; keep the Sabbath; mind your fathers and your mothers; be good, and you will go to heaven." This is not true, and it's not the gospel. The gospel is the same for little children as it is for adults – not "Do this and live," which is after the law that was given by Moses, but "Believe and live," which is according to the grace and truth that came by Jesus Christ. Teachers must impart the gospel if they are to see the salvation of their classes – the gospel, the whole gospel, and nothing but the gospel, for without this, no great thing will be done.

The gospel, the whole gospel, and nothing but the gospel, for without this, no great thing will be done.

And if we want to see the gospel spread abroad in cities as it once was in Geneva or in Scotland under John Knox or in Germany as it was in Luther's day, we must back it up with holy living. After we finish the sermon, people sometimes say, "How about the people who attend there? What about the church members? Are they upright? Are they people you can trust? What about their homes? Do they make good husbands? Are they good servants? Are they kind employers?" People will be sure to question in this way, and if our character is bad, our testimony is ruined. The doctor may advertise, but if the patients are not cured, he is not likely to establish himself as being skilled in his art. The preacher may preach, but if his people do not love the gospel, they trample with their feet what he builds up with his hands.

Yet none of this would produce results unless we added individual personal effort. According to Christ's law, every Christian is to be a minister in his own circle of acquaintances. Every member of the church should spread the faith which was delivered not only to the ministers but also to the saints, to every one of them, that they might share it according to the gift which the Spirit has given them.

Shall I venture a parable? A certain band of men, like knights, had been exceedingly victorious in all their conflicts. They were men of valor and of invincible courage; they had carried everything before them and subdued province after province for their king. But suddenly, in a meeting they proclaimed, "We have at our head a most courageous warrior, one whose arm is strong enough to strike down fifty enemies. Wouldn't it be better if he went to the fight with a few like him, and the other men, who make up the ordinary ranks, stay at home? We would be at greater ease, and our horses would not be so tired and covered with foam. Neither would our armor be battered in returning from the battle, and no doubt great things would be done."

Now, the former champions undertook the task and went to the conflict with fear and trembling, and they fought well, no one could doubt it. To the best of their ability, they conquered their foe and performed great feats. But still, from the moment the scheme was planned and carried out, no city was taken and no province was conquered.

They met together and said, "How is this? Our former reputation is forgotten, and our ranks are broken. Our banners trail in the dust; what is the cause of this?" Then the champion spoke out, "Of course it is so! How did you think that some twelve or fifteen of us could do the work of all the thousands? When you all went to the fight, and every man did his share, we dashed upon the enemy like an avalanche and crushed him beneath our feet. But now that you stay at home and send only a few of us to do all the work, how can you expect that great things should be done?" So each man resolved to put on his helmet and his armor once again and go to the battle, and they gained victory. We must not spare a single man or woman, old or young, rich or poor, but we must each fight for the Lord Jesus according to our ability, so His kingdom may come and His will may *be done in earth, as it is in heaven* (Matthew 6:10).

Chapter 4

Godly Enthusiasm

*Walk worthy of the Lord, pleasing him in
everything, being fruitful in every good
work, and growing in the knowledge of God,
strengthened with all might, according to the
power of his glory unto all patience and long-
suffering with joyfulness.* – Colossians 1:10-11

Whenever any holy enterprise is begun, it is
necessary for it to be watered by the Spirit of
God. Nothing begins well unless it begins in God. It
cannot take root or spring up in hopefulness, unless the
Holy Spirit consecrates it. It will wither like the grass
on the housetops if the heavenly dew of the morning
doesn't fall on it. Likewise, grace is equally needed after
years of growth; there is urgent need of the latter rain,
the shower of revival, in which the old work is fresh-
ened and the lush greenery is restored. Without this
latter rain, the harvest at the end will be disappointing.

The same is true in connection with any labor in which an individual may happen to be engaged. I trust that every believer has found something to do for his Lord and Master. In beginning any Christian work, the novelty produces enthusiasm, which helps the beginner to achieve an easy success. The difficulty for the Christian is seldom in starting the work; the true labor lies in the perseverance, which alone can win the victory. I remind Christians, who have been occupied with a service that the Holy Spirit has given them, of the early rain of their youthful labors, the moisture of which still lingers in their memories, although it may have been followed by long years of drought.

Be encouraged; a latter rain is still possible. Seek it. The fact that you need it so much is a cause for sorrow, but if you really feel your need for it, be glad that the Lord works sacred desires in you. If you did not feel a need for more grace, it would be a reason for alarm. To be conscious that what God did by you in the past has not qualified you to do anything without Him now, and to feel that you lean entirely upon His

The danger of every Christian worker is that of falling into routine and self-sufficiency.

strength as much as ever is to be where God can bless you abundantly. Wait upon Him for the latter rain; ask that He would return and give you ten times more than He has in past years, so that if you have sown in tears, you may come again rejoicing, bringing your sheaves with you.

The danger of every Christian worker is that of

28

falling into routine and self-sufficiency. We are most apt to do what we have been accustomed to do and to do it half asleep. *Therefore let us not sleep, as do others; but let us watch and be sober* (1 Thessalonians 5:6). One of the hardest tasks in the world is to keep the Christian awake on the Enchanted Ground.[4] The tendencies of this present time, and all times, are for people to be lackadaisical and disinterested. The life and the power of our public services and private devotion quickly dissipate; we pray as if we are in a dream, and we praise and preach as if we are sleepwalking. May God be pleased to stir us up, to awaken and quicken us, by sending us the latter rain to refresh His weary heritage.

Today we only have a few giants in grace who rise head and shoulders above the common height – men to lead us in deeds of heroism and efforts of unshakeable faith. After all, the work of the Christian church, though it must be done by all, often owes its existence to single individuals of remarkable grace. In this degenerate time, we are much as Israel was in the days of the judges, for leaders rise among us who are the terror of our foes. If only the church had a race of heroes and our missions could be surrounded with the dignity which marked the church in the early days. If the apostles and martyrs, such as William Carey and Adoniram Judson, could return, what wonders would be worked for us! We have fallen upon a race of dwarfs, and to a great extent we are content to have it so.

---

4   This is a reference to John Bunyan's work, *The Pilgrim's Progress*, where he opens up the discussion for the people of God by explaining the dangers of spiritual lethargy, which he calls the "Enchanted Ground."

There was once a club where the qualification for membership was for men not to exceed five feet in height. These dwarfs held, or pretended to hold, the opinion that they were closer to perfection than others. They argued that primeval men had been far more gigantic than the present race, and therefore, the way of progress caused men to grow less and less, and the human race would become shorter as they perfected themselves. Such a club of Christians could be established and without any difficulty might attain an enormous membership, for the notion is common that our dwarfish Christianity is the standard. Many even imagine that nobler Christians are enthusiasts, fanatical, and hot-blooded, while we are cool because we are wise and indifferent, because we are intelligent.

We must get rid of all this nonsense. The fact is that most of us are inferior to the early Christians, who were persecuted because they were thoroughly Christians, and we are not persecuted because we are hardly Christians at all. They were so earnest in the propagation of the Redeemer's kingdom that they became an irritation in the time they lived. They would not ignore errors. They did not believe they were to hold the truth and allow other people to cling to falsehoods without trying to change their opinions. They preached Christ Jesus in every direction and delivered their testimony against every sin. They denounced the idols and cried out against

They preached Christ Jesus in every direction and delivered their testimony against every sin.

superstition until the world, fearful of being turned upside down, demanded of them, "Is that what you mean? Then we will burn you, lock you up in prison, and exterminate you."

The church replied, "We will accept the challenge and will continue to win the world for Christ." At last, the fire in the Christian church burned out the persecution of an ungodly world.

But we are so gentle and quiet and we do not use strong language about other people's opinions; we let men go to hell out of love for them. We do not want to be confrontational and are not at all fanatical, so the old manslayer has a very easy time of misdirecting people. We don't want to save any sinner who does not particularly want to be saved. We are pleased to say a word to them in a mild way, but we do not speak with tears streaming down our cheeks, groaning and agonizing with God for them. Nor do we thrust our opinions upon them, though we know they are being lost because of their lack of knowledge of Christ crucified. May God send the latter rain to His church, to me, and to you, and may we awaken ourselves and seek after the highest form of urgency for the kingdom of Jesus. May the days come when we don't have to complain that we sow much and reap little, but may we receive a hundredfold reward through the grace of our Lord Jesus Christ.

I have sincerely tried to revive in you an ambition for a higher life and the establishment of a higher standard. Seek to love your Master more; pray to be filled with His Spirit. Do not be mere tradespeople who are

Christianized, but be Christians everywhere – not plated goods, but solid metal. Be servants of Jesus Christ, and *whether therefore ye eat or drink or whatever ye do, do everything for the glory of God* (1 Corinthians 10:31). Serve Him with both your hands and all your heart. Throw your whole force into your Redeemer's service. Live while you live. Don't waste your existence upon common and unproductive ends, but count the glory of Christ to be the only object worthy of your strength, and the spread of the truth the only quest worthy of your mental powers. Spend and be spent in your Master's service. *And whatever ye do, do it heartily, as to the Lord, and not unto men, knowing that of the Lord ye shall receive the reward of the inheritance, for ye serve the Lord Christ* (Colossians 3:23-24).

Chapter 5

Nothing but the Truth

*Or know ye not that to whom ye present your-
selves slaves to obey, his slaves ye are to whom
ye obey, whether of sin unto death or of the
obedience unto righteousness?* – Romans 6:16

The path of obedience is generally a middle path.
*Turn not from it to the right hand or to the left
that thou may be prospered in all the things that thou
doest* (Joshua 1:7).

There is sure to be a right hand, and there is sure
to be a left hand, and both are probably wrong. There
will be extremes on either side. I believe that this is
true in ten thousand things in ordinary life and also
true in spiritual things.

The path of truth in doctrine is generally a middle
one. Men cast such a loving eye on certain tremendous
truths, such as divine sovereignty, the doctrine of elec-
tion, and covenant transactions, that they are quite blind

to all other truths. These great and precious doctrines take up the whole field of their vision, and other equally valuable parts of God's Word are either left unread or twisted into some supposed reconciliation with the first truths. Then others think too much of man and have deep sympathy with the human race. They see man's sin and ruin, and they are charmed with the mercy of God and the invitations of the gospel, which are given to sinners. They become so entranced with these truths in connection with the responsibility of man and man's free agency that they see nothing else and declare all other doctrines to be delusions. If they admit the doctrines of grace to be true, they think they negate the others, but they generally consider them untrue altogether.

I believe that the path of truth is to believe them both – to hold firmly that salvation is by grace and to hold that the ruin of any man is entirely his own fault, to maintain the sovereignty of God and to hold the responsibility of man – to believe in the free agency of both God and man. We desire neither to dishonor God by making Him a puppet to His creatures' will nor to rid man of all responsibility by making him to be a mere machine. Take all that is in the Bible to be true. Never be afraid of any text that is written by the sacred pen. I hope you never wish that any verse could be altered as you turn the pages. I hope you never desire any text to be amended to read a little more Calvinistic or a little more Arminian. Always hold to the truth that your creed must bend to the Bible and not the Bible to your creed; dare to be a little inconsistent or flexible with yourselves if need be, rather than inconsistent with God's revealed truth.

With regard to our words, we generally say too much or too little; we tend to be silent when the wicked are before us or to hurt a good cause through our rashness in defending it. There is a time to speak, and there is a time to be silent; he that judges well will mark his opportunities and take the middle course.

"None but Jesus" must be the constant rallying cry of our spirit.

He will not be rambling with advice that is not required or be silent when he ought to bear testimony for his Master. The same holds true with regard to zeal.

The Christian should not turn to the right or to the left in the matter of his eternal salvation. "None but Jesus" must be the constant rallying cry of our spirit. Some will pull us in one direction and some in another. The wrecker's beacons would entice us upon the rocks in a thousand directions, but let us steer by the sun or by the polar star and not trust the treacherous guides of human fancy. Remember that *no one can lay another foundation than that laid, which is Jesus the Christ* (1 Corinthians 3:11).

So in the matter of faith, let's walk the middle road. Let's not be like those who are presumptuous and refuse to examine themselves, declaring that they must be right. Let's remember that:

> "He that never doubted of his state,
> He may perhaps – perhaps he may – too late."[5]

---

5   William Cowper (1731-1800), *The Poetical Works of William Cowper.*

Let's not fall on the side of constant doubting, imagining that we can never be fully assured but always raising the question:

> "'Tis a point I long to know,
>   Oft it causes anxious thought,
> Do I love the Lord, or no?
>   Am I His, or am I not?"[6]

Let's ask God to guide us in the middle road, where we can say, *I know whom I have believed and am persuaded that he is able to keep that which I have committed unto him against that day* (2 Timothy 1:12). We need to be careful, watchful, and prayerful, as though our salvation depended upon our own diligence, but we must rely on the sure promise and the immutable oath of God, knowing that we stand in Christ and not in ourselves. We are kept by the mighty God of Jacob and not by any power of our own. This middle road, where we don't turn to the right hand of presumption or to the left hand of unbelief, is the path that God would have us walk.

This rule will also hold true with you in your daily life in the matter of your general cheerfulness or attitude. Some people never smile. Dear souls! They pull the blinds down on Sunday. They are sorry that the flowers are so beautiful and think that they ought to have been whitewashed; they almost believe it would be better if the garden beds were a little more neutral in color.

---

6   John Newton (1725-1807), "'Tis a Point I Long to Know."

Don't be deceived with the idea that if a man insists on doing right, by God's grace he will prosper in this world as the consequence. His conscientiousness may actually stand in the way of his prosperity. God does not promise economic gain as a result of doing the right thing. On the contrary, men are often great losers in financial matters by their obedience to Christ.

But the Scripture always speaks to the whole life, where it promises true riches: *the God of our Lord Jesus Christ, the Father of glory, may give unto you the spirit of wisdom and revelation in the knowledge of him; illuminating the eyes of your understanding, that ye may know what is the hope of his calling and what are the riches of the glory of his inheritance in the saints* (Ephesians 1:17-18). If you desire to prosper, stay close to the Word of God and your conscience, and you will have the best prosperity. You might not see it in a week or a month or a year, but you will enjoy it at some time. I have seen hundreds who have asked my advice as to what they should do. I almost always noticed that those who attempt to follow a policy of doing as little wrong as possible, but maybe just a little, always blunder from one mishap to another. Their whole life is a life of compromises, sins, and miseries.

But I have noticed others who have come straight and cut the cords that entangled them. They have said, "I will do the right thing, even if I die for it." Though they have had to suffer, there was always a turn somewhere, and eventually they've said, "I thank God, in spite of all my crosses and losses, that I was led to be faithful to my convictions, for I am a happier man, if not a richer man." In some cases they've actually become richer men, for even in this world honesty is the best policy. It is a very simple way of looking at it, but right and righteousness do get the respect and the esteem of men in the end. The thief, though he takes a short way to get rich, takes such a dangerous way that it does not pay, but he who walks straight along the narrow road will find it to be the shortest way to the best kind of prosperity, both in this world and in the next.

One good brother, whose shoelace I am not worthy to untie, said that when he went up the Rhine, he never looked at the rocks, or the old castles, or the flowing river; he was too taken up with other things! But to me, nature is a mirror in which I see the face of God. I delight to gaze abroad and "Look through nature up to nature's God."[7]

But that was all unholiness to him. I do not understand that kind of thing. I have no sympathy with those who look upon this material world as though it were a very wicked place with no trace of the divine hand, no proof of divine wisdom, and no manifestations of divine care. I believe we should delight ourselves in the works of God, find much pleasure in them, and get drawn to God Himself by considering His works. For, *every good gift and every perfect gift is from above and comes down from the Father of lights* (James 1:17). That concept of strict seriousness that lacks the ability to see the beauty of God around us is one extreme.

But there are others who are all jokes and hilarity

---

7   Alexander Pope (1688-1744), "Of the Nature and State of Man with Respect to Happiness." *http://www.bartleby.com/40/2804.html.*

and still profess to be Christians, but they cannot live without the same amusements as those who are not Christians. They go from one party to another; they are never comfortable unless they are making jokes and taking part in all the pranks and rowdiness of the world. Ah, the previous example is a pardonable weakness with much that is commendable, but this rabble-rouser is a detestable one, of which I can say nothing that is good.

The Christian should steer between the two. He should be cheerful, but not outlandish. He should be sustained and joyful under all circumstances; he should readily have a kind word for others. He should be a man among men as the Savior was who sat at the banquet and feasted and rejoiced with those who rejoiced but remained heavenly minded

Some men act in such a way that from morning until night they can think of nothing but business.

in it all. He should feel that a joy in which he cannot have Christ with him is no joy, and places of amusement where he cannot take his Lord with him are not places of amusement, but scenes of misery to him. He should be cheerful, happy, and rejoicing, but at the same time, he should display a deep solemnity of spirit that removes everything that is sacrilegiously light and trifling far from him.

By the same rule, conduct your business. Some men act in such a way that from morning until night they can think of nothing but business. I mourn over some Christians who did not know when they had had enough. When they had no more need of gain, they still launched out into something else that would take all opportunities for serving God's cause and all time for reflection and thought away. This brought barrenness and leanness into their souls. Others do not work enough at their callings. They are at a sermon when they ought to be behind the counter, or they are enjoying a prayer meeting when they ought to be mending their husband's stockings. They go out preaching in the villages when they should be earning money to pay their creditors. There are extremes, but the true Christian is diligent in business and fervent in spirit as he seeks to combine the two. The believer would be like one of old, a man *just and devout*, not having one duty smeared with the blood of another duty.

Chapter 6

Be Strong and Courageous

*Only be thou strong and very courageous that
thou mayest keep and do according to all the
law, which Moses my slave commanded thee;
turn not from it to the right hand or to the left
that thou may be prospered in all the things
that thou doest.* – Joshua 1:7

Joshua was highly favored with promises, which were
given to him by God. They were broadly comprehen-
sive and exceedingly encouraging, but Joshua would not
say to himself, "These covenant engagements will surely
be fulfilled; therefore, I can sit still and do nothing." On
the contrary, because God had decreed that the land
should be conquered, Joshua was to be diligent to lead
the people to battle. He was not to use the promise as a
shelter upon which his idleness might indulge, but as a
girdle to gird up his loins for future activity.

To urge us to action, let's always remember and

respect the gracious promises of our God. If we were to say within ourselves, "God will not desert His people, so let's venture into sin," we would be sinning most detestably. We are almost equally wicked if we whisper in our minds, "God will fulfill His own decrees and give the souls of His redeemed as a reward to His Son Jesus; therefore, let's do nothing and avoid zealous Christian service." This is not proper language for true children. This is the talk of the apathetic ignorant or mere pretenders, who mock God while they pretend to reverence His decrees. By the oath, by the promise, by the covenant, and by the blood that sealed it, we are exhorted continually to be at work for Christ, because we are saved that we may serve Him in the power of the Holy Spirit with heart and soul and strength.

Joshua was especially exhorted to continue in the path of obedience. He was the captain, but the great Commander-in-Chief gave him his marching orders. Joshua was not left to his own fallible judgment or fickle fancy, but he was to do according to all that was written in the book of the Law. So is it with us who are believers. We are not under the law but under grace. Yet there is a gospel rule that we are bound to follow, and the law in the hand of Christ is a delightful rule of life to the believer.

Only be thou strong and very courageous that thou mayest keep and do according to all the law, which Moses my slave commanded thee (Joshua 1:7). When you heard the words *Only be thou strong and very courageous*, you assumed that some great undertaking was to be performed, and that was correct, for all accomplishments are comprehended in that one declaration, *that thou mayest keep and do according to all the law, which Moses my slave commanded thee.* The highest feat of the Christian life is to obey Christ. No man shall perform such an undertaking unless he has learned the rule of faith, been led to rest upon Christ, and advanced to obedience in a strength which is not his own, but which he has received from the indwelling Holy Spirit.

The world sees obedience as a mean-spirited thing and speaks of rebellion as freedom. We have heard men say, "I will be my own master; I shall follow my own will." To be a freethinker and a free liver seems to promote the world's glory; but if the world could be reasonable and convict itself of its foolishness with the indisputable proof that is provided, it would never be difficult to prove that a reviler of the obedient is a fool. Consider the world's own military rule. Isn't the man who is thoroughly obedient to the captain's command presumed to be the boldest and best soldier?

A story of the old French wars has been repeated hundreds of times. A sentinel was set to keep a certain position, and at nightfall as he is pacing, the emperor himself came by. He did not know the password, so immediately the soldier stopped him. "You cannot pass," he said.

"But I must pass," said the emperor.

"No," replied the man, "if you were the little corporal in grey himself, you could not go by" (meaning the emperor). Thus, the emperor was held in check by order. The vigilant soldier was rewarded later, and all the world said that he was a brave fellow.

Now, from that instance, and hundreds more, we learn that obedience to superior commands that are carried out in the midst of hazards is one of the highest proofs of courage that a man can possibly give. The world itself gives its endorsement to this. Then certainly, it is not a horrible and sneaky thing for a man to obey Him who is the Commander-in-Chief of the universe, the King of Kings and Lord of Lords. He who does the right and true thing in the midst of ridicule is a bolder man than he who flings himself before the cannon's mouth for fame. Yes, to persist in precise obedience throughout life may take more courage than even the martyr demonstrates when he gives himself to be burned at the stake.

In Joshua's case, full obedience to the divine command involved innumerable difficulties. The command to him was that he should conquer the whole land for the favored tribes, and to the best of his ability, he did it, but he had to besiege cities that were protected with walls and fight with monarchs whose warriors came to battle in iron chariots, armed with scythes. The first conflicts were terrible. If he had not been a bold and able soldier, he would have put up his sword and fled from the battle, but the spirit of obedience sustained him. Though you and I have no Hivites and Jebusites to kill, no cities to pull down, and no chariots of iron to encounter, we will still find it no easy thing to continue on the path of Christian consistency.

Moreover, Joshua not only had difficulties to face, but he also made many enemies through his obedience. As soon as Jericho had fallen and Ai had been taken, we read of first one alliance of kings and then of another, whose objective was to destroy the power of Joshua. These kings knew that he would crush them, if they did not crush him.

Now, the Christian man is in a similar plight. He will be sure to make enemies. He will try not to make enemies; but if he does the right things, believes the truth, and carries out the honest things, he will lose every earthly friend. He will count it a small loss, however, since his great Friend in heaven will be friendlier and reveal Himself more graciously than ever.

In his obedience, Joshua needed much courage, because he had undertaken a task that involved long years of perseverance. After he had captured one city, he had to go on to attack the next fortress. The days were not long enough for his battles. He bid the sun to stand still, and the moon stopped. Even when that long day had passed, he still had his sword in his hand the next morning. Joshua was like one of those old knights who slept in their armor. He was always fighting. His sword must have been quite chipped, and his armor must have been blood-red. He had a lifelong enterprise before him.

Such is the life of the Christian, a warfare from end to end. As soon as you are washed in Christ's blood and clothed in His righteousness, you must begin to carve your way through your enemies, right up to the eternal throne. Every foot of the way will be disputed; Satan will not yield an inch to you. You must continue to fight every day. *He that shall endure unto the end, the same shall be saved* (Matthew 24:13). The beginner, who begins in his own strength, soon comes to an end; but he who is encircled with divine grace, with the Spirit of God within him, determines to stand firm until he has overcome the last foe. He never leaves the battlefield until he has heard the words, *Well done, thou good and faithful slave* (Matthew 25:21).

Let the man who says that the Christian's life is common and devoid of manliness go and learn wisdom before he speaks, for of all men the persevering believer is the most manly. You who boast about yourself and your courage in sinning, you give in to the Enemy. You are a cringing cur; you turn tail upon the Enemy and flee. You court the friendship of the world and don't have courage enough to do the right and true thing. You have been humiliated by Satan and your own passions, and you conceal your own cowardice. You are corrupt enough to call the brave Christian man a coward. Out with you for adding lying to your other vices!

Often if we follow Christ, we will need to be brave as we face the world's customs. This is true in commercial businesses. Husbands will find this so even in connection with their wives and children, if they are unsaved. Children find this to be so in their schools. Retailers find it so in the marketplace. He who wants to be a true Christian needs to have a stout heart.

There is a story of Dr. Adam Clarke, which shows the

courage that the youthful Christian sometimes needs. While he was in a shop in a town, they were preparing for the annual fair, and some rolls of cloth were being measured. One of them was too short, and the master said, "Come, Adam, you take that end, and I will take the other, and we can pull it and stretch it until it is long enough." But Adam chose not to listen or use his hands for his master's dishonest order, and in the end he flatly refused. Then the master said, "You will never make a tradesman; you are good for nothing here; you had better go home and take up something else."

That type of thing may not be done today, for men do not generally cheat in such an open way now, but they cheat in more deceitful fashions. The records of the bankruptcy court will tell you what I mean. Bankruptcies one after another for the same person are generally doubled-distilled thievery – not old-fashioned theft like that which once brought men to the gallows, but something worse than highway robbery and burglary. Sometimes the genuine Christian will have to put his foot down and say, "No, I cannot, and I will not be mixed up with such a thing as that." He may have to be this blunt to his master, his father, or his friend, even though he desires to gain the respect of those who may be of great assistance to him in life. But if it is your duty to do the right thing, do it even if the skies fall. Do it if poverty stares you in the face. Do it if you are turned into the streets tomorrow. You will never be a loser with God

> It is your duty to do the right thing, do it even if the skies fall.

in the end, and if you have to suffer for righteousness' sake, you are blessed! Count yourselves to be happy that you have the privilege of making any sacrifice for the sake of conscience, for today we don't have the power to honor God as they did who went to prison or to the stake. Therefore, let's not reject other opportunities that are given to us to show how much we love the Lord and how faithfully we desire to serve Him. Be courageous to do what the Lord Jesus bids you to do in all things, and let men judge you to be an idiot if they will. You will be one of the Lord's champions, a true soldier of the cross.

The world says, "We must not be too precise." Hypocritical world! The world would be glad to get rid of God's law altogether, but since it doesn't dare to say that point-blank, it whines with the most sickening of all hypocrites, "We must not be too particular or too nice."

As someone said to an old Puritan once, "Many people have ripped their consciences in halves; couldn't you just make a little nick in yours?"

"No," he said, "I cannot, for my conscience belongs to God."

"We must live, you know," said a money-loving shopkeeper, as his excuse for doing what he could not otherwise defend.

"Yes, but we must also die," was the reply, "and therefore we must do no such thing." There is no particular necessity for any of us living. We are probably better dead, if we cannot live without doing wrong.

The very essence of obedience lies in exactness.

Probably your child would still do what you told him even though he was sometimes disobedient. It would be in the little things that commendable obedience would appear. Let the world judge for itself. Here is an honest man. Do people say of him, "He is such an honest man that he would not steal a horse"? No, that would not prove him to be very honest; but they say, "He would not even take a pin that did not belong to him." That is the world's own description of honesty, and when it comes to obedience to God, it is the same. Here is a merchant, and he boasts, "I have a clerk who is such a good accountant that you would not find a mistake of a single penny in six months' reckoning." It would not have meant much if he had said, "You would not find a mistake of ten thousand pounds in six months' reckoning." And yet if a man stands firm on little things and is exact and particular, the world charges him with being too inflexible, too strict, too straitlaced, while all the time he is demonstrating that the essence of honesty and of correctness is exactness in little things.

Chapter 7

According to Your Faith

And he died for all that those who live should not live from now on unto themselves, but unto him who died and rose again for them. – 2 Corinthians 5:15

Nothing is impossible to the man who knows how to affect heaven by wrestling intercession. When we have seen one, two, ten, or twenty penitents converted, and when we have sometimes been heartily thankful that a hundred have been added to the church in a month, should we have been satisfied? Shouldn't we have felt that the prayer, which effected the conversion of a hundred, might have been answered with the conversion of a thousand if it had been more earnest? Why not? I don't know why our great city shouldn't be shaken from end to end with gospel truth a year from now. You might say, "We don't have enough ministers."

But God can make them. He can find ministers for

His truth – yes, if He willed it, among the very outcasts of the earth. He can take the worst of men, the vilest of the vile, and change their hearts and make them preach the truth, if He pleases. We are not to look to what we have. The witness of the senses only confuses those who would walk by faith. See what He did for the church in the case of Saul of Tarsus. God just went up to the devil's army, took out a ringleader, and said to him, "Now, sir, you preach the gospel which once you despised." And who preached it better? Why, I should not wonder if before long in answer to prayer we see the ritualistic clergy preaching the gospel! Who can tell? The Roman priests may do it and repeat the tale of Luther and Melanchthon.[8] Weren't Luther, Melanchthon, Calvin, and their comrades brought out of papal darkness to show light to the people? We have heard with our ears; why don't we see with our eyes the mighty works of God? The Lord can find His men where we know nothing about them. John the Baptist pointed to the banks of the Jordan and said, *God is able to raise up children unto Abraham of these stones*, and as He could do then, so He can do now (Matthew 3:9). Let's not despair. If we will only pray for it, our heavenly Father will deny His children nothing. Come in simplicity of heart and *according to your faith be it unto you* (Matthew 9:29).

> He can take the worst of men, the vilest of the vile, and change their hearts and make them preach the truth, if He pleases.

8   Philip Melanchthon (1497-1560) was a German theologian and Luther's successor as leader of the Reformation in Germany.

Consider two different persons. They are both alive, but one of them lies in bed. He wakes, but he says with the sluggard, "You woke me too soon; I must sleep more," and when he gets up, he gazes around with a vacant stare and strange bewilderment. He has no energy; he is listless.

We say of him, "What a lifeless creature he is! He is living, but with such little vitality!"

Now you see another man. His sleep is short; he wakes soon; he is out to his business and takes down the shutters. He stands behind the counter, waiting upon his customers. He is active; he is here, there, and everywhere, and nothing is neglected. His eyes are wide open, his brain is active, his hands are busy, and his limbs are all nimble. What a different man from the first. You are glad to get this second man to be your servant; he is worth ten times the wages of the first. There is life in both, but what a difference there is between them! The one is eagerly living; the other is dragging out a wearisome existence. And how many Christians there are of this sort! They wander in on a Sunday morning, sit down, get their hymnbook out, listen to the prayer without joining in it, and hear the sermon, but they might as well not have heard it, go home, get through the Sunday, and go in to their business. With them there is never any secret prayer for the conversion of men, no trying to talk to children, or servants, or friends, about Christ. They have no zeal, no holy jealousy, no flaming love, and no generosity. This is too true a picture of a vast number of professing Christians. How I wish it were not so!

On the other hand, we see another kind of man – one that is renewed in the spirit of his mind. As the apostle Paul instructed, *And be not conformed to this age, but be ye transformed by the renewing of your soul that ye may experience what is that good and well pleasing and perfect will of God* (Romans 12:2). Though he has to be in the world, his main thoughts are how to use the world to promote the glory of Christ. If he goes into business, he wants to make money, so he might have something to give for the spread of the gospel. If he meets with friends, he tries to share a word for his Master, and whenever he gets an opportunity, he will speak or write, but he will be aiming to do something for Him who has bought him with His precious blood. If it were right to mention names, some in this congregation are alive, working until their bodies seem scarcely strong enough for the real vitality and energy of their souls. These are the cream of the church, the choice of the flock, the true men, and the true daughters of Jerusalem.

So, it is not the great man who is filled with learning who will achieve great work for God; it is the man who, however small his ability, is filled with force and fire. He rushes forward in the energy which heaven has given him to accomplish the work. He is the man who has the most intense spiritual life and real vitality at its highest point of tension. He lives with all the force of his nature for the glory of God. Put these three or four things together, and I think you have the means of success.

Chapter 8

God's Laborers

For this we both labour and suffer reproach,
because we trust in the living God, who is
the Saviour of all men, specially of those that
believe. – 1 Timothy 4:10

What kind of men does the Master mean to use? They must be *laborers.* The man who does not make hard work of his ministry will find it very hard work to answer for his idleness at the last great day. A gentleman who wants an easy life should never think of occupying the Christian pulpit. He would be out of place in that position, and when he gets there, the only advice I can give him is to get out of it as soon as possible. If he will not leave the position voluntarily, I recall the language of Jehu concerning Jezebel, *Throw her down*, and think the advice applicable to a lazy minister (2 Kings 9:33).

An idler has no right in the pulpit. He is an instrument

of Satan in damning the souls of men. The ministry demands brain labor; the preacher must throw his thoughts into his teaching, and read and study to keep his mind in good shape. He must not weary the people by telling them the truth in a stale, unprofitable manner with nothing fresh from his own soul to give force to it. Above all, he must put heart-work into his preaching. He must feel what he preaches; it must never be an easy thing for him to deliver a sermon. He must feel as if he could preach his very life away before the sermon is done. There must be soul-work in it as well; the entire man must be stirred up to the effort. The whole nature that God has given him must be concentrated with all its energy upon the work in hand. Such men we want. To stand and drone out a sermon in a kind of articulate snoring to a people who are somewhere between awake and asleep must be wretched work. I wonder what kind of excuse will be given by some men for having habitually done this. To proclaim a dry creed, teach certain doctrines, and expound and enforce them logically, but to never deal with men's consciences, upbraid them for their sins, tell them of their danger, or invite them to a Savior with tears and entreaties is a powerless work. What will become of such preachers? God have mercy upon them! We want laborers, not loiterers. We need men on fire, and I beg you to ask God to send them. The harvest cannot be reaped by men who will not labor; they must take off their coats and go at it in their shirtsleeves. I mean they must discard their dignities and get to Christ's work as if they meant it, like real harvestmen. They must sweat at their work, for nothing in the harvest field can be done without the sweat of the face, or in the pulpit without the sweat of the soul.

But what kind of laborers are required? They must be men who will go down into the wheat. You cannot reap wheat by standing a dozen yards off and beckoning to it; you must go up close to the standing stalks, and every reaper knows that. And you cannot move people's hearts and bring men to Christ by imagining you are a superior being who condescends when he shakes hands with a poor man. There is a genteel order of preaching, which is as ridiculous as reaping with a lady's ivory-handled pocketknife with kid gloves on. I do not believe God will ever bless it. Get among the wheat like men in earnest! God's servants should feel that they are one with the people; whoever they are, they should love them, claim kinship with them, feel glad to see them, and look them in the face and say, "Brother." Every man is a brother of mine; he may be a very bad one, but in spite of that, I love him and long to bring him to Jesus. Christ's reapers must get among the wheat.

Christ's reapers must get among the wheat.

See what the laborer brings with him. It's a sickle. His communications with the corn are sharp and cutting. He cuts right through, cuts the corn down, and casts it on the ground. The man whom God intends to be a laborer in His harvest must not come with soft and delicate words and flattering doctrines concerning the dignity of human nature, the excellence of self-help, and the earnest endeavors to correct our lapsed condition. Such mealymouthedness (groveling) God might curse, for it is the curse of this age.

The honest preacher calls a sin "a sin," and a spade "a spade," and says to men, "You are ruining yourselves; while you reject Christ you are living on the borders of hell, and before long you will be lost to all eternity. There will be no mincing the matter; you must escape from the wrath by coming to faith in Jesus or be driven forever from God's presence and from all hope of joy." The preacher must make his sermons cut. He must not file off the edge of his scythe for fear it should hurt somebody.

The gospel is intended to wound the conscience and go right through the heart with the purpose of separating the soul from sin and self, as the corn is divided from the soil. Our objective is to cut the sinner down, for all the attraction of the flesh, its glory, and its excellence must be slain; the man must be as one dead before he can be saved. Ministers who do not cut deep are not worth their weight in salt. God doesn't send the man who never troubles men's consciences. Such a man may be a donkey treading down the corn, but a reaper he certainly is not. We want faithful ministers; pray to God to send them.

But then a laborer has only begun when he cuts the corn; much more is needed. As he cuts, he lets the corn fall onto his arm, and then he lays it along in rows; afterwards he binds it together into bundles that it may be gathered. So the laborer whom God sends into the field must be a gathering laborer; he must be one who brings God's people together, comforts those who mourn, and picks those up who were cut down by the sharp sickle of conviction. He must bind the saints together and edify them in their most holy faith.

Remember that the laborer's work is never done in harvest time until he sees the corn housed. Until it is stacked or put into a barn, his toil is not over. And, if God has anointed the Christian minister to His work, he never stops caring for souls until they get to heaven. He is like Mr. Great-heart with Christiana and Mercy and the children; he goes with them from the City of Destruction all the way to the River Jordan.[9] If he could, he would go through the river with them. It is his business to march in front with his shield, to meet the dragons and giants with his sword, and to protect the little ones. His job is to be tender to them as a shepherd with the lambs and a nurse with her children, for he longs to present them to his Master in the end and say, "Here am I, and the children that Thou hast given me."

We are to pray to the Lord, for it is the Lord's business. Only the Lord can send us the right men. He has a right to send whomever He pleases, for this is His harvest, and a man may employ whomever he wants in his own field. It would be in vain to appeal to anybody else. It is of no use to appeal to bishops to find us laborers. God alone has the making of ministers and the raising up of true workers; therefore, the petition

---

9   This is another allusion to John Bunyan's *The Pilgrim's Progress.* Mr. Great-heart is sent by the interpreter as a guide and protector for Christiana, a young woman named Mercy, and Christiana's four sons. Mr. Great-heart is a man of strong faith, courage, and faithfulness.

must be addressed to Him. *Pray ye therefore the Lord of the harvest, that he will send forth labourers into his harvest* (Matthew 9:38).

The first three petitions of the Lord's Prayer contain this prayer: *Our Father who art in the heavens, Hallowed be thy name. Thy kingdom come. Thy will be done in earth, as it is in heaven* (Matthew 6:9). Doesn't that mean,

We ought to pray continually to the Lord of the harvest for a supply of earnest laborers.

"Lord, send forth men who may teach this world to hallow Your name, that through Your Spirit's power they may be the means of making Your kingdom come and causing Your will to be done in earth as it is in heaven"? We ought to pray continually to the Lord of the harvest for a supply of earnest laborers.

Notice the expression used in Matthew 9: *that he will send forth labourers.* The Greek is much more forceful; it implies that He would push them forward and thrust them out. The same word is used for the expulsion of a devil from a possessed man. It takes great power to drive a devil out; it will take equal power from God to drive a minister out to his work.

I always say to young fellows who consult me about the ministry, "Don't be a minister if you can help it," because if the man can help it, God didn't call him, but if he cannot help it, and he must preach or die, then he is the called man. May the Lord push men out, thrust them out, drive them out, and compel them to preach the gospel. Unless they preach by a divine compulsion, there will be no spiritual urgency in their ministry for the hearts of others. *Pray ye therefore the Lord of the harvest, that he will send forth labourers into his harvest.*

Our Lord said, *into his harvest.* I like that, because the harvest is not ours. If that harvest shall perish, it is our heavenly Father's harvest that perishes. This makes it weigh upon my soul. If they told me that the harvest of some harsh, overbearing tyrant was perishing, I might say, "Let it! If he had it, what good would it be to him or anybody else? He grinds the faces of the poor. Who wants to see him rich?" But when it is our gracious God, our blessed loving Father, one cannot bear the thought, and yet Jesus puts it before us that it is God's harvest that is perishing for lack of reaping.

Suppose an angel took you upon his wing and poised you in mid-space miles above the earth where you could look back down with clear eyesight. Imagine that you rested there, and the world revolved before you for twenty-four hours. The sunlight gradually came upon all parts of the world and made certain colors visible, which marked where there was grace, where there was idolatry, where there was atheism, and where there was legalism. You would grieve to see that only here and there in our world were the bright marks of the grace of God like little drops of dew, but various shades of darkness would show you that the whole world was in the power of the Wicked One.

And if the vision changed, and you saw the two hemispheres spread out like a map and transformed into a cornfield, all white for the harvest, how sad you would be to see a few men reaping their little patches, doing the best they can, but the great mass of the corn is untouched by the sickle. You would see acres of land where no ears had been reaped since the foundations of the world. You would be grieved to think that God's corn is spoiling; men whom He has made in His own image and made for immortality are perishing for lack of the gospel. *Pray ye*: that is the stress of the whole text – *Pray ye therefore the Lord of the harvest, that he will send forth labourers into his harvest* that these fields may not rot before our eyes.

"But I shall never preach," a man may say. If you do not preach, you can serve God some other way. Couldn't you start a prayer meeting in your house? Some of you live in different parts of the city; couldn't you find new interests? Do something for Jesus. Some of you, good women, couldn't you get young women together and talk to them about the Savior? Yes, but perhaps some brother has been smothering in his heart a desire to go into the missionary field. Do not quench the Spirit. *But watch thou in all things, labour, do the work of an evangelist, fulfill thy ministry* (2 Timothy 4:5). You may be missing your vocation while trying to suppress that desire. I would rather you burst into fanaticism and become fools in enthusiasm than remain in a dead coolness, caring little for the souls of men.

What do Christian people think about today? If they hear about Japan, they say, "Oh, we shall have a new trade there." But do they say, "Who among us can go to Japan to tell them of the gospel?" Don't you think that merchants and soldiers and sailors and people who trade with distant parts of the world are the very persons to spread the gospel? Shouldn't a Christian man say, "I will try to find a trade for myself, which will bring me into contact with a class of persons that need the gospel, and I will use my trade as the means for reaching people for Christ. Since hypocrites use religion for gain, I will make my work useful to my ministry."

"Oh," says one, "we can leave that to the society." God bless the society, but I was going to say, "Smother the society, rather than allow it to smother personal effort." We want our godly merchants, working men, soldiers, and sailors everywhere to feel, "I cannot have a proxy in the shape of a society to do this for me; in the name of God, I will do it myself and have a share in this great battle." If you cannot labor yourself, the society is the grandest thing conceivable, for you may help others in that way; but the main cry from Christ is that you yourself should go into the highways and byways and compel as many as you find to come in to the gospel feast.

Chapter 9

The Power of the Gospel of Christ

Let no man despise thy youth, but be thou an example of the faithful in word, in conversation, in charity, in spirit, in faith, in purity. – 1 Timothy 4:12

Often while men sketch out imaginary designs, they have missed actual opportunities. They would not build because they could not erect a palace; they therefore shiver in the winter cold. They wouldn't wear homespun clothes, for they looked for scarlet and fine linen; before long, they had none. They were not content to do a little, so they did nothing. It is vain to pray for an extensive revival of religion and comfort each other in the hope of it, if meanwhile our zeal, enthusiasm, and sparkle dissipate. With the highest expectations and the largest longings, our proper plan is to imitate the woman of whom it is written, *She has*

done what she could (Mark 14:8). By laboring diligently in whatever may be within our reach, we follow
Solomon's precept: *Whatever thy hand finds to do, do
it with all thy might* (Ecclesiastes 9:10). While believers
are zealously doing what God enables them to do, they
are on the high road to abundant success; but if they
stand idle all day, gazing after wonders, their spiritual
inadequacy will come upon them as an armed man.

Andrew is the picture of what all disciples of Christ
should be. This first successful Christian missionary was
a sincere follower of Jesus. While so many will naively
thrust themselves into the offices in Christ's church,
having no concern for the glory of His kingdom, it
will always be needful to repeat that warning: *Unto the
wicked God saith, What part hast thou to declare my
statutes?* (Psalm 50:16). Men who have never seen the
beauties of Emmanuel are not fit persons to describe
them to others.

Andrew was earnest for the souls of others, though
he was just a young convert. He appears to have seen
Jesus as the Lamb of God one day and to have found
his brother Peter the next. Far be it from us to forbid
you, who only yesterday found joy and peace, to exert
your new zeal and youthful passion. No, don't delay,
but make haste to spread the good news that is now
so fresh and full of joy to you. Yes, the advanced and
the experienced should deal with the faultfinding and
the skeptics, but you, young as you are, may find some
with whom you can share – some brother like Simon
Peter or some sister dear to you, who will listen to your
straightforward tale and believe your simple testimony.

Andrew was a new disciple, a commonplace disciple, a man of average capacity. He does not seem to be the brilliant character that Simon Peter his brother turned out to be. Andrew's name occurs throughout the life of Jesus Christ, but no notable incident is connected with it. Later in life, he no doubt became a most useful apostle, and according to tradition, he sealed his life's ministry by death on a cross; yet in the beginning, Andrew was an ordinary believer, one of common standard with nothing remarkable. Andrew became a useful minister, and thus it is clear that servants of Jesus Christ are not to excuse themselves from endeavoring to extend the boundaries of His kingdom by saying, "I have no remarkable talent or singular ability."

Are we, as servants of God, to be measured by mere oratorical ability?

I disagree with those who denounce ministers with insignificant gifts, sneering at them as though they shouldn't fill the pulpit at all. Are we, as servants of God, to be measured by mere oratorical ability? Is this after the fashion of Paul, when he renounced the wisdom of words lest the faith of the disciples should stand in the wisdom of man and not in the power of God? He said, *My speech and my preaching was not with enticing words of human wisdom, but in demonstration of the Spirit and of power* (1 Corinthians 2:4). If you blotted out all the minor stars from the Christian church and left nothing but those of the first magnitude, the darkness of this poor world would increase sevenfold. How often the outstanding preachers, who are the church's delight, are brought into the church by those of common standing, even as Simon Peter was brought by Andrew! Who can tell what might have become of Simon Peter if it had not been for Andrew? Who can say that the church would ever have possessed a Peter if she had closed the mouth of Andrew? And who can put their finger upon the brother or sister of inferior talent and say, "These must hold their peace"? No, if you only have one talent, use it more zealously. God will require it of you.

Then he who had received the one talent came and said, Lord, I knew thee that thou art a hard man, reaping where thou hast not sown and gathering where thou hast not scattered; therefore, I was afraid and went and hid thy talent in the earth; behold, thou hast what is thine. His lord answered and said unto him, Thou wicked and slothful slave, thou knewest that I reap where I did not sow and gather where I have not scattered; therefore, it was expedient for thee to have put my money to the bankers, and then at my coming I should have received mine own with interest. Take, therefore, the talent from him and give it unto him who has ten talents. (Matthew 25:24-28)

Don't let your brothers hold you back from making use of your talent. If you are only like a glowworm's lamp, don't hide your light, for there is an eye needing to see that light, a heart looking for comfort from your faint gleam. Shine and the Lord will accept you.

Every single professor of the faith of Christ is bound to do something for the extension of the Redeemer's kingdom. I wish that everyone, whatever his talents, would be like Andrew in promptness. As soon as he's a convert, he becomes a missionary; as soon as he's taught, he begins to teach. I would have them be like Andrew, persevering as well as prompt. He first finds Peter – that is his first success, but who knows how many he found afterwards? Throughout a long life of usefulness, Andrew probably brought many stray sheep to the Redeemer, yet certainly that first one would be among the dearest to his heart.

The object of the soul winner is not to only bring men to an outward religiousness. Little will you have done for a man if you make the Sabbath-breaker into a Sabbath-keeper and leave him a self-righteous Pharisee. Little will you have done for him if you persuade him to be a mere user of a form of prayer with his heart not in it. You only change the form of sin in which the man lives; you prevent him from drowning in the salt water, but you throw him into the fresh; you take one poison from him, but you expose him to another. The fact is that if you really serve Christ, your prayer and your zeal will follow the person who has become the object of your attention, until by grace he places his faith in Jesus Christ and accepts eternal life as it is found in the atoning sacrifice. Anything short of this may have usefulness for this world but will be useless for the world to come. May your aim be to bring men to Jesus, not to bring them to baptism, or to the meeting-house, but to bring them to His feet who alone can say, *Thy sins are forgiven. . . . Thy faith has saved thee; go in peace* (Luke 7:48, 50).

To bring men to Jesus, you can proceed with the

next step – that of instructing them or finding a way for them to be informed concerning the gospel. It is an astonishing thing that while the light of the gospel is abundant to us, it is only partially distributed in much of the country. When I have described my own hope in Christ to two or three on a train, I have recognized that my listeners are perfect novices in spiritual things. The faces of many intelligent Englishmen have shown their astonishment when I explained the doctrine of the substitutionary sacrifice of Christ. Some of these people have even attended their parish church from their youth but were totally ignorant of the simple truth of justification by faith.

Yes, and some who have been to dissenting places of worship do not seem to have grasped the fundamental truth that no man is saved by his own doings, but that salvation is gained by faith in the blood and righteousness of Jesus Christ. This nation is saturated to the throat in self-righteous doctrine, and the Protestantism of Martin Luther is generally unknown. The truth is held by as many as God's grace has called, but the great outlying world still talks of doing your best and then hoping in God's mercy and maybe legal self-confidence. All of this while the master doctrine that he who believes in Jesus is saved by Jesus's finished work is sneered at as fanaticism or attacked as leading to licentiousness. Tell it, then, tell it on all sides; take care that no one

> The statement of the gospel has often proved enough in God's hand to lead a soul into immediate peace.

under your influence is left in ignorance of it. I can bear personal witness that the statement of the gospel has often proved enough in God's hand to lead a soul into immediate peace.

Not many months ago, I met with a lady who held religion and the popery in high regard, but as I spoke with her, I was delighted to see how interesting and attractive the gospel was to her. She confessed that she enjoyed no peace of mind as the result of her religion, and she never seemed to have done enough. She had an elevated concept of priestly absolution, but it had been unable to calm her spirit. She feared death and thought God was terrible; even Christ was an object of awe rather than love.

When I told her that whoever believes on Jesus is perfectly forgiven and that I knew I was forgiven, I saw a new framework for thinking take life in her mind. I told her I was as sure of forgiveness as of my own existence, and I feared neither life nor death, for it would be the same to me, because God had given me eternal life in His Son. She said, "If I could believe that, I would be the happiest person in the world." I did not deny her conclusion; instead, I claimed to have proved its truth, and I have reason to believe that the little simple talk we had has not been forgotten. You cannot tell how many may be in bondage for lack of the simplest possible instruction on the plainest truths of the gospel of Jesus Christ.

Many may be brought to Christ through your example. Believe me, there is no preaching in this world like the preaching of a holy life. It shames me sometimes, and weakens me in my testimony for my Master, when I realize that some professors of religion are a disgrace not only to their religion but also even to common morality. It makes me feel as though I must speak with bated breath and trembling knees, when I remember the damnable hypocrisy of those who thrust themselves into the church of God and by their abominable sins bring disgrace upon the cause of God and eternal destruction upon themselves. In the proportion that a church is holy, its testimony for Christ will be powerful. Oh, if only the saints were immaculate, our testimony would be like fire among the stubble, like the flaming firebrand in the midst of the sheaves of corn. If the saints of God were less like the world, more disinterested, more prayerful, and more godlike, the armies of Zion would shake the nations, and the day of the victory of Christ would surely dawn.

Chapter 10

Doing All as unto the Lord

Slaves . . . not to be seen as only pleasing men,
but as the slaves of the Christ, doing the will
of God from within, with good will doing
service as to the Lord and not to men, know-
ing that whatever good thing anyone does, the
same shall they receive of the Lord, whether
they are slaves or free. – Ephesians 6:5-8

The Holy Spirit does not ask us to leave our professions in order to serve the Lord. He does not ask us to forsake the domestic relationships which make us husbands or wives, parents or children, masters or servants. He does not suggest that we put on a peculiar robe and seek the seclusion of a hermit or the retirement of a monastic or cloistered life. Nothing of the kind is hinted at, but He asks the servant to continue in his or her service *with good will doing service.* Our great Captain would not have you hope to win the

73

victory by leaving your post. He would want you to remain in your trade, calling, or profession and serve the Lord there, doing the will of God from the heart in common things. This is the practical beauty of our holy faith – that when it casts the devil out of a man, it sends him home to bless his friends by telling them of great things the Lord has done for him. Grace does not transplant the tree, but invites it to overshadow the old house as before and bring forth good fruit where it is.

Grace does not make us unearthly, though it makes us unworldly. True religion distinguishes us from others, even as our Lord Jesus was separate from sinners, but it does not shut us up or hedge us around as if we are too good or too tender for the rough usage of everyday life. It does not put us in the saltbox and shut the lid down, but it throws us in among our fellow men for their good. Grace makes us the servants of God, while we are also the servants of men. It enables us to do the business of heaven, while we are attending to the business of earth; it sanctifies the common duties of life by showing us how to perform them in the light of heaven. The love of Christ makes the lowliest acts glorious. As the sunlight brightens a landscape and sheds beauty over the most common scene, so does the presence of the Lord Jesus. The Holy Spirit renders the offices of domestic service as divine as the worship that is presented upon the sea of glass before the eternal throne by the angels of heaven.

Whether we are servants or masters, whether we are poor or rich, let's take this as our rallying cry: *as to the Lord and not to men* (Ephesians 6:7). May this be the engraving of our seal and the motto of our coat of arms from this point forward – the constant rule of our life and the sum of our motives. In advocating this gracious goal for our lives, let me say that if we are enabled to adopt this motto, it will first influence our work itself, and secondly, it will elevate our spirit concerning that work. Let me add that if the Lord shall be the all-in-all of our lives, it is only what He has a right to expect and what we are under a thousand obligations to give to Him.

If we do indeed live *as to the Lord*, we must live wholly to the Lord. The Lord Jesus is an all-encompassing Master. He has said, *No one can serve two masters*, and we will find it so (Matthew 6:24). He will have everything or nothing. If He is our Lord, He must be sole Sovereign, for He will not brook a rival.[10] The conclusion for you as a Christian is that you are bound to live for Jesus and for Him alone. You cannot have a co-master or even a secondary objective or divided goal; if you divide your heart, your life will be a failure. As no dog can follow two hares at one time, or he will lose both, certainly no man can follow two contrary objectives and hope to secure either of them. A servant of Christ must be a concentrated, focused man. His affections should be bound up into one affection, and that affection should not be set on things on the earth, but on things above. *Set your sight on things above, not*

If we do indeed live as to the Lord, we must live wholly to the Lord.

---

10   "Brook a rival" is a Japanese proverb, probably taken from ancient Chinese. It means "two great men cannot stand together." *www. languagerealm.com/japanese/japaneseproverbs_ri.php.*

on things on the earth (Colossians 3:2). His heart must not be divided, or it will be said of him as of those in the book of Hosea, *Their heart has wandered; now they shall be found guilty* (Hosea 10:2). The chamber of the heart is too narrow to accommodate the King of Kings and the world, or the flesh, or the devil, at the same time.

In the service of God, we should use great care to accomplish our very best, and we should feel a deep longing to please Him in all things. In the trade of paper staining, a man flings colors upon the paper to make common wall decorations, and by rapid processes acres of paper can be quickly finished. Suppose the paper stainer laughed at a prominent artist when he had covered such a small space, because he had stippled and shaded a tiny piece of his picture by the hour. Such ridicule would itself be ridiculous. Now the world's way in religion is the paper stainer's way, the daubing way; there is plenty of it, and it is quickly done. But God's way, the narrow way, is a careful matter; there is little of it, and it requires thought, effort, watchfulness, and care. But note how precious the work of art is when it is done and how long it lasts.

You will not wonder why a man spends his time on the painting; even so, true godliness is acceptable to God and endures forever. Therefore, it repays the earnest effort of the man of God exceedingly. The miniature painter has to be very careful of every touch and tint, for a very little spot may spoil his work. Let our life be a miniature painting. *With fear and trembling* let it be worked out (Philippians 2:12). We are serving the

Holy God, who requires reverence of them that come near to Him; let us mind what we do.

Our blessed Master never made a faulty stroke when He was serving His Father; He never lived a careless hour or spoke an idle word. He lived a careful life; even the night watches were not without the deep anxieties as He poured forth His prayer to God. If you and I think that the first opportunity that comes to us will do to serve our God, we make a great mistake and grossly insult His name. We must have a very low understanding of His infinite majesty if we think that we can honor Him by doing His service halfheartedly or in a slovenly style. No, if you will live *as to the Lord, and not unto men*, you must watch each motion of your heart and life, or you will fail in your purpose (Colossians 3:23).

Our work for Jesus must be the outgrowth of the soil of the heart. Our service must not be performed as a matter of routine; there must be vigor, power, freshness, reality, eagerness, and warmth about it, or it will be good for nothing. No fish ever came upon God's altar, because it could not come there alive; the Lord wants none of your dead, heartless worship. You know what is meant by putting heart into all that we do; demonstrate it by your lives. A work which is to be accepted by the Lord must be heart-work throughout, not a few thoughts of Christ, and a few chill words, and a few chance gifts, but as the heart beats, so must we serve God. It must be our very life. We are not to treat our religion as though it were a sort of hobby farm, which we were willing to keep going but not to make much of, while our chief thoughts are focused on the home farm of self and the world with its gains and pleasures. Our Lord will be *aut Caesar aut nullus* – either a Caesar (ruler) or a nothing. My Master is a jealous husband; He will not tolerate a stray thought of love elsewhere, and He thinks it scorn that they who call themselves His beloved should love others better than Himself. Such impurity of heart can never be permitted; let us not dream of it.

What a mean and beggarly thing it is for a man to do his work well only when he is watched. Such oversight is for boys at school and mere hirelings. You never think of watching noble-spirited men. As Paul told the Philippians, *as ye have always hearkened, not as in my presence only, but now much more in my absence, work out your own saving health with fear and trembling* (Philippians 2:12).

> What a mean and beggarly thing it is for a man to do his work well only when he is watched.

When a young apprentice sets about to copy a picture, his master stands over him and looks over each line, for the young rascal will grow careless and spoil his work, or he will play around if he is not looked after. Did anybody dream of supervising Raphael and Michelangelo to keep them at their work? No, the master artist requires no eye to urge him on. Popes and emperors came to visit the great painters in their studios, but did they paint better because these grandees gazed upon them? Certainly not. Perhaps they did worse in the excitement or the worry of the visit.

They had regard for something better than the eye of pompous personages. So the true Christian wants no eye of man to watch him. Some pastors and preachers may be better for being looked after by bishops and presbyters, but fancy a bishop overseeing the work of Martin Luther and trying to quicken his zeal. Or imagine a presbyter looking after Calvin to keep him sound in the faith. Oh no, gracious minds outgrow the governance and stimulus that come from the oversight of mortal man. God's own Spirit dwells within us, and we serve the Lord from an inward principle, which is not fed from without. A real Christian has a prevailing sense that God sees him, and he does not care who else may set his eye upon him; it is enough for him that God is there. He has little respect for the eye of man; he neither courts it nor dreads it. Let the good deed remain in the dark, for God sees it there, and that is enough. Or, let it be blazoned in the light of day to be pecked at by the critics, for it little matters who disapproves as long as God approves. This is the heart of a true servant of Christ: to escape from being an eye-servant to men by becoming an eye-servant to God in a glorious sense.

What about wages? Is that the motive of a Christian? Yes, in the highest sense, for the greatest of the saints, such as Moses, *had respect unto the recompense of the reward*, and we would be despising the reward that God promises to His people if we have no respect for it (Hebrews 11:26). Respect for the reward that comes from God kills the selfishness that is always expecting a reward from men. We can postpone our reward, and

we can be content to be misunderstood and misrep-
resented instead of receiving present praise. We can
postpone our reward, and we can endure and labor
on without success. When the reward does come, how
glorious it will be! An hour with Jesus will make up
for a lifetime of persecution! One smile from Him will
repay us a thousand times over for all disappointments
and discouragements.

Chapter 11

A Great Leader and Good Soldiers

*For thou art my rock and my fortress; there-
fore for thy name's sake thou shalt lead me
and guide me.* – Psalm 31:3

What wonders men can do when they are influenced by enthusiastic love for a leader! The
troops of Alexander the Great marched thousands of
miles on foot, and they would have been utterly wearied
had it not been for their zeal for Alexander. He led them
forth conquering and to conquer. Alexander's presence
was the life of their valor and the glory of their strength.
If there was a very long day's march over burning sands,
one thing they knew – that Alexander marched with
them. If they were thirsty, they knew that he thirsted
too, for when one soldier brought a cup of water to the
king, he put it aside, thirsty as he was, and said, "Give
it to the sick soldier."

Once it happened that they were loaded with the loot that they had taken, and each man had become rich with garments and wedges of gold. When they marched slower with so much to carry, the king feared that he would not overtake his enemy. Having a large quantity of the loot that was his own share, he burned it all before the eyes of his soldiers and asked them to do the same, so they might pursue the enemy and win even more. "Alexander's portion lies beyond!" he cried, and seeing the king's own spoils on fire, his warriors were content to give up their gains and share with their king. He did himself what he commanded others to do; in self-denial and hardship, he was a full partaker with his followers.

After this fashion our Lord and Master acts toward us. He says, "Renounce pleasure for the good of others. Deny yourself, and take up your cross. Suffer, though you might avoid it; labor, though you might rest, when God's glory demands suffering or labor from you. Have I not set you for an example?" *For ye know the grace of our Lord Jesus Christ, that, though he was rich, yet for your sakes he became poor that ye through his poverty might be enriched* (2 Corinthians 8:9). He stripped Himself of all things that He might clothe us with His glory. When we heartily serve such a Leader as this and are fired up by His spirit, then murmuring, and complaining, and weariness, and fainting of heart are altogether fled; a divine passion carries us beyond ourselves.

I believe great numbers of working men always consider how little they can possibly do to earn their wages. The question with them is not, "How much can we give for the wage?" but "How little can we give? How little work can we do in the day without being discharged for idleness?" Many men say, "We must not do all the work today, for we shall need something to do tomorrow. Our masters will not give us more than they can help; therefore, we will not give them more than we are obliged to."

This is the general spirit on both sides, and as a nation, we are going to the dogs because that spirit is among us. We shall be more and more beaten by foreign competition if this spirit is cultivated. Among Christians, such a notion cannot be tolerated in the service of our Lord Jesus. It never works for a minister to say, "If I preach three times a week, it is quite as much as anybody will expect of me; therefore, I shall do no more." It will never be right for you to say, "I am a Sunday school teacher; if I get into the class at the last minute and stop as soon as the time is over, I do not need to look after the boys and girls through the week. I cannot be bothered with them; I will do as much as I am required to do, but no more." In one particular town, the grocer's wife cut a plum in two, for fear there would be an ounce too much in the parcel, so the folks called her Mrs. Split-plum. Yes, there are many split-plums in religion. They do not want to do more for Jesus than is absolutely necessary. They would like to give good weight, but they don't want to be convicted of doing too much.

When we feel we are doing service for our Lord Jesus Christ, we adopt a more liberal scale. Then we do not calculate how much ointment will suffice for His feet, but we give Him all that our box contains. Is this what you say: "Here, bring the scales, because this ointment costs a great deal of money; we must be economical. Watch every cent, every ounce and grain, for the oil is costly"? If this is your cool manner of calculation, your offering is not worth a fig. Not so with that daughter of love of whom we read in the gospels, for she broke the box and poured out all the contents upon her Lord. *Why was this ointment not sold for three hundred denarius and given to the poor?* cried Judas (John 12:5). He was the one who said this, and you know, therefore, the worth of the observation. Christ's servants delight to give so much that it is thought wasteful, for they feel that when they have done extravagantly for Christ, they have only begun to show their hearts' love for His dear name. Thus, the elevating power of the spirit of consecration lifts us up above the wretched stinginess of mere formality.

"Is the work good enough?" said one man to his servant.

The man replied, "Sir, it is good enough for the price, and it is good enough for the man who is going to have it." When we serve men, we may perhaps rightly judge in this way, but when we come to serve Christ, is anything good enough for Him? Could our zeal know no respite, could our prayers know no pause, and could our efforts know no relaxation? Could we give all we have of time, wealth, talent, and opportunity; could we die a martyr's death a thousand times; wouldn't He, the Beloved of our souls, deserve far more? Yes, He does deserve more. Therefore, self-congratulation is banished forever. *Now we are free from the law of death in which we were held, that we might serve in newness of Spirit, and not in the oldness of the letter* (Romans 7:6). When you have done all, you will feel that it is not worthy of the matchless merit of Jesus, and you will be humbled at the thought. Thus, while doing all for Jesus stimulates zeal, it also fosters humility, a happy blending of useful effects.

The resolve to do all as unto the Lord will elevate you above that craving for recognition, which is a disease with many. It is a sad fault in many Christians that they cannot do anything unless the whole world is told about it. The hen in the farmyard lays an egg and feels so proud of the achievement that she must cackle about it. Everybody must know about that one poor egg, until the whole country resounds with the news. Some professors are like this; their work must be published, or they can do no more. "Here have I," said one, "been teaching in the school for years, and nobody ever thanked me for it. I believe that some of us who do the most are the least noticed, and what a shame it is." But if you have done your service unto the Lord, you would not talk like that, or we would suspect you of having other motives. The servant of Jesus will say, "I do not want human notice. I did it for the Master; He noticed me, and I am content. I tried to please Him, and I did please Him. Therefore, I ask no more, for I have gained my end. I seek no praise from men, for I fear the breath of human praise could tarnish the pure silver of my service."

If you seek the praise of men, you will in all probability fail in the present, and certainly, you will lose it in the future. *For do I now persuade men or God? or do I seek to please men? for if I yet pleased men, I should not be the slave of Christ* (Galatians 1:10). Many men are more ready to criticize than to commend, and to hope for their praise is to seek for sugar in a root of wormwood. Man's way of judging is unjust and seems fashioned on purpose to blame all of us one way or another. One brother sings bass, and the critics say, "Oh yes, a very fine bass voice, but he could not sing soprano." Another excels in soprano, and they say, "Yes, yes, but we prefer a tenor." When they find a tenor, they blame him because he cannot take the bass. No one can be candidly praised, but all must be savagely criticized. What will the great Master say about it? Won't He judge like this: "I have given this man a bass voice, and he sings bass, and that is what I meant him to do. I gave that man a tenor voice, and he sings tenor, and that is what I meant him to do. I gave that man a soprano voice, and he sings soprano, and that is the part I meant him to take. All the parts blended together make up sweet music for My ears."

Wisdom is justified of all her children, but folly blames them all round (Luke 7:35). How little we ought to care about the opinions and criticisms of our fellow men when we recall that He who made us what we are and helps us by His grace to act our part will not judge us after the manner in which men complain or flatter, but will accept us according to the sincerity of our hearts. If we feel, "I was not working for you; I was working for God," we shall not be as wounded by our neighbors' remarks. The nightingale charms the ear of night. A fool passes by and declares that he hates such distracting noises. The nightingale sings on, for it never entered the little minstrel's head or heart that it was singing for critics. It sings

> "We don't live for you, O men; we live for our Lord."

because He who created it gave it this sweet ability. So may we reply to those who condemn us: "We don't live for you, O men; we live for our Lord." In this way, we escape the discouragements that come of uncharitable misunderstanding and jealous criticism.

If those you seek to bless are not saved, you have not failed altogether, for you did not teach or preach with the winning of souls as the final condition of your work. You did it with the view of pleasing Jesus, and He is pleased with faithfulness, even where it is not accompanied with success. Sincere obedience is His delight, even if it leads to no apparent result. If the Lord should set His servant to plow the sea or sow the sand, He would accept his service. If we should have to witness for Christ's name to sticks and stones, and our hearers should be worse than blocks of marble, we may still be filled with contentment, for we will have done our Lord's will. What more do we want? To plod on under apparent failure is one of the most acceptable of all works of faith, and he who can do it year after year is assuredly well pleasing unto God. *Therefore, be ye not unwise, but understanding of what the will of the Lord is* (Ephesians 5:17).

We will have to leave our work soon, and we are apt to fret about it. The truth is that we will go on with our work forever if our service is pleasing to the Lord. We will please Him up yonder even better than we do here. And what if our enterprise here should seem to end, as far as man is concerned? We have done it unto the Lord, our record is on high, and therefore it is not lost. Nothing that is done for Jesus will be destroyed; the flower may fade, but its essence remains; the tree may fall, but its fruit is stored; the cluster may be crushed, but the wine is preserved; the work and its place may pass away, but the glory, which it brought to Jesus, shines as the stars forever and ever.

A proper sense of serving the Lord would exalt all our service beyond conception. Think of working *for Him* – for Him, the best of masters, before whom angels count it glory to bow. Work done for Him is in itself the best work that can be done, for all that pleases Him must be pure and lovely, honest and of good report. Work for the eternal Father and work for Jesus are works which are good and only good. To live for Jesus is to be swayed by the noblest of motives. To live for the incarnate God is to blend the love of God and the love of men in one passion. To live for the ever-living Christ is elevating to the soul, for its results will be most enduring. When all other work is dissolved, this shall abide. Men speak of painting for eternity, but we will serve for eternity.

Soon all worlds will behold the superiority of the service of Christ, for it will bring with it the most blessed of all rewards. When men look back on what they have done for their fellows, they see small recompense for a patriotic life. The world soon forgets its benefactors. Many men have been supported in youth by the applause of men, and then in their old age, they have been left to starve to their graves. He who scattered gold at first, begs pennies in the end. The world called him generous while he had something to give, and when he had given all, it blamed his indiscretion. He who lives for Jesus will never have grounds to complain concerning his Lord, for He did not forsake His saints.

> *The work of each one shall be made manifest, for the day shall declare it because it shall be revealed by fire; the work of each one, whatever sort it is, the fire shall put it to test. If the work of anyone abides which he has built thereupon, he shall receive a reward. If anyone's work shall be burned, he shall suffer loss, but he himself shall be saved, yet so as by fire.* (1 Corinthians 3:13-15)

Man never regretted what he did for Jesus, except that he may regret that he has not done ten times more. The Lord will not leave His old servants. *O God, thou hast taught me from my youth and until now; I shall manifest thy wondrous works. Now also when I am old and grayheaded, O God, forsake me not* – such was the prayer of David, and he was confident of being heard (Psalm 71:17-18). Such may be the confidence of every servant of Christ. He may go down to his grave untroubled; he may rise and enter the solemn state of the eternal world without a fear, for service for Christ creates heroes to whom fear is unknown. *In this the charity with us is made perfect, that we may have confidence in the day of judgment, that as he is, so are we in this world* (1 John 4:17).

Chapter 12

Sunday School Ministry

*And let us not be weary in well doing, for
in due season we shall reap if we faint not.*
– Galatians 6:9

Sunday school work is *well-doing.* How can it be
otherwise, for it is an act of obedience. I trust that
you teach because you call Jesus your Master and Lord,
and you wish to fulfill the great command, *Go ye into
all the world and preach the gospel to every creature*
(Mark 16:15). You find children to be creatures, fallen
creatures, but still lovable little things, full of vigor,
life, and glee. You see them as a fundamental part of
the race, and you conclude that your Master's command applies to them. You are not like the disciples
who wanted to hold them back, for you have learned
from their mistake, and you remember the words of
their Master and yours, *Suffer the little children to come
unto me and forbid them not* (Matthew 19:14). You also

know that *out of the mouths of babes and sucklings hast thou ordained strength because of thine enemies*, so you are sure He included the little ones in the general commission when He said, *preach the gospel to every creature* (Psalm 8:2; Mark 16:15).

You are doubly sure that you are obeying His will because you have specific directions which relate to the little ones, such as *feed my lambs* and *train up a child in the way he should go; even when he is old, he will not depart from it* (John 21:15; Proverbs 22:6). You know that it is our duty to preserve a testimony in the world, and therefore you are anxious to teach the Word to your children that they may teach it to their children, so from generation to generation the Word of the Lord may be known. Whether the task is pleasant or tiresome to you, it is not yours to hesitate but to obey. The love that has redeemed you also compels you. You feel the touch of the sacred hand upon your shoulder, the hand that was pierced, and you hear your Redeemer say, *As my Father has sent me, even so send I you* (John 20:21). Because of that sending, you go to the little ones in obedience to His will. He who obeys is doing well, and in this sense, your service among the little ones is well-doing.

It is also well-doing because it brings glory to God. We must continue to receive from God, who is the great fountain of goodness and blessing, as He permits us to make Him some return. As the dewdrop reflects the beam from the great sun that adorns it, so may we make the light of our great Father sparkle before the eyes of men. May our lives be as the rivers that run into the sea from wherever they originate. Whenever we attempt what promotes the divine glory, we are well-doing. When we make Jehovah's grace known, when we work in accordance with His purposes of love, when we speak the truth that honors His beloved Son, and whenever the Holy Spirit bears witness of the eternal truths of the gospel through us, there is well-doing towards God. We cannot increase His intrinsic glory, but through His Spirit we can make His glory seen more widely; teaching children the fear of the Lord so they may serve Him and rejoice in His salvation is among the best ways to make His glory known.

And who can doubt that Sunday school work is well-doing towards man? The highest form of charity is to teach our fellow man the gospel of Jesus Christ. You can give bread to your friend, but when he has eaten, it is gone. If you give him the Bread of Life, however, it abides with him forever. You can give him lots of bread, but in due time he will die, as his fathers have before him. If you give him the bread of heaven, and he eats, he will live forever. God has enabled you to provide him with immortal food, even Jesus, who is that bread from heaven. Jesus said, *I AM the living bread which came down from heaven; if anyone eats of this bread, they shall live for ever* (John 6:51). What a blessing it is to a man if you are the instrument of changing his heart, emancipating him from vice, and freeing him to holiness. To lead a soul to Christ is to

> The highest form of charity is to teach our fellow man the gospel of Jesus Christ.

lead it to heaven. To deliver the gospel to the sons of men is a noble part of benevolence. If possible, this benevolence is a higher kind when you deliver the truth of God to children, for prevention is better than a cure; it is better to prevent a life of vice than to rescue that life from depravity. The earlier a soul has light, the shorter its night of darkness; likewise, the earlier in life that salvation comes to the heart, the greater its benefit. To receive the dew of grace while we are still in the dew of youth is a double blessing.

Your work is one of well-doing of the most thorough and radical kind, for you strike at the very root of sin in the child by seeking his regeneration. You desire, by the grace of God, to win the heart for Christ at the beginning of life, and this is the best of blessings. I hope you are not among those who only hope to see your children converted when they are grown up. I hope you are not satisfied to let them remain in their sins while they are children. I hope that you pray for the conversion of children as children and are working to that end by the Spirit's gracious aid. I don't know of any service more fitting to engage the angels of heaven, if they could be permitted to undertake it. Surely, if they could teach the gospel to mankind and have their choice of students, they might pass by those who are already hardened in sin and only have their old age to offer to Christ; those angels might prefer to gather the young whose day is just dawning for Him. We should not set one work against another, but we might count ourselves happy if our circle is among the young. Let us gather the rosebuds for Jesus. Let us bring the virgin in her earliest beauty to Him and the young man in his first vigor, before sin and age have spoiled them of their charms. Let us find those who can give Him a whole life and honor Him from dawn until evening. Oh, it is glorious to have such work for Jesus! Go to your youthful charges and rejoice in your work, for it is well-doing.

When I had a little garden of my own, I planted mustard and cress. I went the next morning to see if it was sprouting and was not satisfied to wait for the due season. I turned the mound over, and I daresay I halted the growth of the seed by my impatience. It is quite possible for teachers to make the same mistake by an unbelieving hurry, expecting to reap tomorrow what they have sown today. Immediate fruit may come, for God works marvelously, but whether it does or not, your plain duty is to sow. You shall reap, but meanwhile you must be satisfied to go on sowing, sowing, and sowing, even to the end. Reaping is your reward, but sowing is your work – sowing, sowing, always sowing, until the hand is paralyzed, and the seed basket is carried on another arm. Well-doing by sowing the seed is your work.

You will be tempted to grow weary. Teaching children is hard work. Some good souls seem born to teach, do it splendidly, and enjoy it; to others it is a tough labor. Some are by nature exceedingly inept at it, but I do not think they should excuse themselves by that fact; they should educate themselves into loving the work. Many people around us are inept at anything that causes them to perspire, but we call them lazy and goad them on. It is no new thing for men to attempt to avoid the army by pretending to be in bad health, but we cannot have cowardly evasion in Christ's army. We must be ready for anything and everything. We must compel ourselves to duty when it goes against the grain. When it is a clear duty, obedience must master our aversion. I have no doubt that any teaching is very toilsome work to some, but it has to be done all the same. I delight to hear you speak with enthusiasm of the privilege of teaching children, and I fully believe in it, but I know also that it requires no small degree of self-denial on your part – self-denial for which the church does not always give you due credit. To continue from Sunday to Sunday, drilling a little biblical knowledge into those noisy boys and trying to calm down those giddy girls is no easy entertainment or pretty pastime. It must be toilsome, and therefore it is not difficult to become weary.

Teachers may tire quicker because the work lasts year after year. I admire the veterans of your army. There ought to be an Old Guard as well as new regiments. Why leave this work to young beginners? Didn't David say, *Come, ye children, hearken unto me; I will teach you the fear of the LORD*, when he was in the prime of life (Psalm 34:11)? Why, then, do so many cease to teach when they are best qualified to do so?

Don't many older people have a gentleness and an impressiveness which peculiarly qualify them to catch the attention of the young? As they know more by experience than most of us, shouldn't they be more ready to impart instruction? It was always my delight to sit at my grandfather's feet when he told about his experience in the grace of God. When he was eighty years old or more, his witness to the faithfulness of God was worth going many miles to hear. Scores of older men and women have life stories that ought to be told among children; with their loving ways and cheerful manners, they would be an asset to any school for the children's sake, and their weight and wisdom would be an incalculable benefit to the teachers.

Die working if your mental and physical vigor will permit. Still, the many years' labor must make the worker weary, and more so if the work is allowed to become monotonous, as it is in some schools. You might go to the same dingy room and sit on the same chair before the same class of boys. It is true the boys are not the same boys, for though the proverb says, "Boys will be boys," I find that they will *not* be boys, but that they will be men. But still, one boy is much like another boy, so the class is always the same. The lessons vary, but the truth is the same, and the work of teaching is like the sowing of seed – very much the same thing over and over again. Lovers of change will hardly find in regular Sunday school work a field for their fickleness. The text says, *let us not be weary* (Galatians 6:9). Are you tired out? How long have you been teaching? A thousand years? You smile, and I smile too, and say, Do not be weary with any period of service short of that. Our Lord deserves a whole eternity to be spent in His praise, and we hope to spend it with Him; therefore, let us not be weary with the few years which constitute the ordinary life of man.

Chapter 13

Hard Work and its Reward

*Now he that plants and he that waters are
one although each one shall receive his
own reward according to his own labour.
For we are labourers together with God.*
– 1 Corinthians 3:8-9

Do you suppose our negligence in Christian work arises from being very low in grace? As a rule, you cannot get out of a man what is not in him. You cannot teach your class and do your work vigorously if you have lost inward vigor. You cannot minister before the Lord with the anointing of the Holy One if the Holy Spirit is not upon you. If you are not living near to God and in the power of God, then the power of God will not go forth through you to the children in your care. I think we should realize that when we become discontented and downhearted, we are out of sorts spiritually. Let's say to ourselves, "Come, my soul! What ails you? This faint heart is a sign that you are not healthy. Go to the Great Physician and obtain medicine that will strengthen you. Come, be a man. Get rid of these notions! Get rid of your idleness! The reaping time will come, so thrust in the plow."

Another reason we become downhearted is found in the coldness and indifference of our fellow Christians. We see others doing the Lord's work carelessly, and when we are on fire ourselves, we find them to be cold as ice. We get among people in the church who don't seem to care whether the souls of the children are saved or not, and thus we are apt to be discouraged. The idleness of others should be an argument for being more diligent ourselves. If our Master's work is suffering at the hands of our fellow servants, shouldn't we try to do twice as much to make up for their deficiencies? Shouldn't those loafers be warnings to us, so we don't take on that same lukewarm condition? To argue that I should be a sluggard because others waste time is poor logic.

Sometimes, though I am ashamed to mention it, I have heard of teachers becoming weary from lack of appreciation. Their work has not been sufficiently noticed by the pastor and praised by the superintendent, and sufficient notice has not been taken of them and their class by their fellow teachers. I will not say much about this cause of weakness, because it is such a deplorable flaw that it is quite below a Christian. Appreciation! Do we expect it in this world? The Jewish nation despised and rejected their King, and even if we were as holy as the Lord Jesus, we might still fail to be rightly judged and properly esteemed. What does it matter? If God accepts us, we don't need to be disheartened, though all should pass us by.

Perhaps, however, the work itself may suggest another excuse for being weary. It is hard work to sow on the highway and among the thorns – hard work to be casting good seed upon the rock year after year. Well, if I had worked hard for many years and was enabled by the Holy Spirit, I would say, "I shall not give up my work because I have not yet received a reward. I perceive that in the Lord's parable, three sowings did not succeed, and yet the one piece of good ground paid for all. Perhaps I have gone through my three unsuccessful sowings, and now is my time to enjoy my fourth, in which the seed will fall upon good ground." It is a pity, when you have had some years of rough work, to give it all up now. Why, now you are going to enjoy the sweets of your former labor. It would be a pity, just when you have mastered your class and prepared the way for a blessing, for you to run away from it. There is much less difficulty for you to overcome compared to what you have already overcome. He who has passed so many miles of a rough voyage will not have to go over those miles again; don't let him think of going back. Indeed, to go back in this pilgrimage would be shameful, and as we have no armor for our back, it would be dangerous. Putting our hand to this plow and looking back will prove that we were unworthy of the kingdom. If

> It would be a pity, just when you have mastered your class and prepared the way for a blessing, for you to run away from it.

there are a hundred reasons for giving up your work of faith, there are fifty thousand for going on with it. Though there are many arguments for fainting, there are far more arguments for persevering. Though we might be weary and sometimes feel like quitting, let us *wait for the LORD* and renew our strength, and we will *mount up with wings as eagles,* forget our weariness, *and be strong in the Lord and in the power of His might* (Isaiah 40:31; Ephesians 6:10).

We have abundant encouragement in the prospect of reward. *In due season we shall reap if we faint not* (Galatians 6:9).

The reaping time will come. Our chief business is to glorify God by teaching the truth, whether souls are saved or not, but I still challenge the statement that we may preach the gospel for years and years, and even our whole lifetime, and have no results. They say, "Paul *may* plant and Apollos *may* water, but God gives the increase." I would like them to find that passage in the Bible. In my English Bible it says, *I* [Paul] *have planted, Apollos watered, but God gave the increase* (1 Corinthians 3:6). There is not the slightest intent to insinuate that when Paul planted and Apollos watered, God would arbitrarily refuse the increase. All the glory is claimed for the Lord, but honest labor is not despised.

I do not say that the same relationship exists between teaching the truth and conversion as there is between cause and effect, such that they are invariably connected. But I will maintain that it is the rule of the kingdom that they should be connected through the power of the Holy Spirit. Some causes will not produce effects because certain obstacles intervene to prevent it. A person may teach the gospel in a bad spirit, and that would spoil it. A person may teach only part of the gospel, and he may present it the wrong way. God may bless it somewhat, but the good man may greatly retard the blessing by the mistaken manner in which he delivers the truth.

As a rule, the truth of God, prayed over and spoken in the fear of the Lord with the Holy Spirit dwelling in the man who speaks it, will produce the effect that is natural to it. As the rain doesn't climb up to the skies, and the snowflakes never take wing to rise to heaven, so neither shall the Word of God *return unto me* [God] *void, but it shall accomplish that which I please* (Isaiah 55:11). We have not spent our strength in vain. Not a verse taught to a little girl, a text dropped into the ear of a careless boy, an earnest warning given to a stubborn young sinner, or a loving farewell to one of the senior girls will be without glory given to God. Taking it all together, though this handful of seed may be eaten by the birds, and that other seed may die on the hard rock, as a whole, the seed will spring up in sufficient abundance to plentifully reward the sower and the giver of the seed. We know that our labor is not in vain in the Lord. Go to your classes with this persuasion: "I shall not labor in vain or spend my strength for nothing." *According to your faith be it unto you* (Matthew 9:29). Take a little measure, and you shall have it filled with the manna of success; but take a great omer, and in its fullness you shall have abundance. Believe in the power of the truth you teach. Believe in the power of Christ about whom you speak. Believe in the omnipotence of the Holy Spirit, whose help you have called for in earnest prayer. Go to your sowing, and plan on reaping.

Let us not be weary . . . for in due season we shall reap (Galatians 6:9). *We* shall reap. It is not, "We shall do the work, and our successors shall reap after we are gone." We should be very pleased if our successors reap, and no doubt such is often the case. But *we* shall reap too. Yes, I shall have my sheaves, and you will have yours. The plot which I have toiled and wept over shall yield me my sheaves of harvest, and I shall personally gather them. I shall reap. "I never thought much of myself as a teacher," someone said. "I always feel that I am hardly competent, and I notice that the superintendent has only trusted me with the little children, but I am so glad to hear that I shall reap. I shall reap. I will have a dear little one, saved in the Lord, to be my portion." I pray that if you have never reaped, you begin to hope.

I shall reap.

You teachers who are not punctual, if you do not come in time, you do not care whether you reap or not. But I speak to punctual teachers and to earnest teachers, for if you are not earnest, you will never reap; punctual, earnest, prayerful teachers shall reap. Some teachers do not attempt reaping, and they will not enjoy it. But I am speaking now to real, hardworking, earnest Sunday school teachers who give their hearts to the work and have seen no results. According to the text, you shall reap. Come, my persevering comrades, let's not be discouraged: *in due season we shall reap,* even we. You will have your share with others. Though you feel as though you must give it up, you shall reap. After sowing all this while, don't cease from labor when reaping time is so near.

If I were a farmer and gave up my farm, it should be before I sowed my wheat; but if I had done all the plowing and the sowing, I would not say to my landlord, "There are six weeks and then comes harvest; let another tenant come in to harvest." No, no. I would want to stop, harvest the wheat, and take it to market. I would want to have my reward. So, you who have been discouraged should wait for your profit. *In due season we shall reap if we faint not.* We who have exercised the least faith and endured the most searchings of heart and groaning and crying before the Lord, we also *in due season shall reap if we faint not.*

What reward can equal the conversion of these young immortals? Isn't it the greatest delight that we can enjoy on earth, next to communion with our Lord, to see these little ones saved?

Taking the Sunday school, however, on a broad scale, I think your reward partly lies in rearing up a generation of worship-loving people. We cannot reach the great masses of the city whatever we may do. If you go into evangelistic assemblies, you will soon detect from the manner of the singing that most of the people are accustomed to sacred songs. We do not know how to get at the great tens of thousands, but you do. You reach them while they are young, and you send them home to sing their hymns to their fathers, who will not come and sing them. The children go home and tell their mothers all about Jesus, so the children in the city are the missionaries. They are Christ's heralds to the families where ministers would be totally shut out. You are training them up, and if you do this work well, we will need more places of worship and more ministers, for the people will come to the house of prayer. I charge you to recognize the connection between your senior classes and the church and see if this is not so. When that day arrives, there will be a grand time for the preachers of the Word.

> Shall they read material to direct them to be highwaymen and thieves, or shall they read to become servants of the living God?

In some villages and towns, you will scarcely find a single person absent when the house of God is open! They all go to a church or to the meetinghouse. But it is not so in our city. We have hundreds of thousands who forget the Sabbath. I fear we have more than a million of our fellow citizens who go so seldom to a place of worship that they may be said to be habitually absent. It will be a grand thing if you can change all this and give us church-going millions.

I believe that there will be another reward for you, namely, that of saturating the whole population with religious truth. All children are now supposed to learn to read. Shall they read material to direct them to be highwaymen and thieves, or shall they read to become servants of the living God? Much of that will depend upon you. You will take care to introduce your children to interesting but sound literature before other interests.

Your boys must read, and if you are the teacher of a boy who reads *Jack Sheppard*, you will be sadly to blame if he continues to delight in such an abomination.[11] I trust that your leaven will leaven the whole lump of our country, that you will be the means of improving the moral tone of society, and as generation follows generation, I trust we shall see a nation bright with religious knowledge, devout with religious thought, and in all things exalted by justice and truth.

---

11   William Harrison Ainsworth, *Jack Sheppard,* a novel based on the
      real life of the eighteenth-century criminal Jack Sheppard.

Chapter 14

Our Time with the Scriptures

For the word of God is alive and efficient and sharper than any twoedged sword, piercing even to the dividing asunder of soul and spirit, and of the joints and marrow, and is a discerner of the thoughts and intents of the heart. – Hebrews 4:12

I am afraid that this is a magazine-reading age, a newspaper-reading age, a periodical-reading age, but not so much a Bible-reading age as it ought to be. In Puritan times, men had a scant supply of literature, but they found a whole library in the one Book, the Bible. And how they did read the Bible! But how little of Scripture there is in modern sermons compared with the sermons of those masters of theology, the Puritan priests and clergymen! Almost every sentence of theirs seems to relate to a text of Scripture – not only the one they are preaching on, but many others as well are set in a new light as the discussion proceeds. They introduce blended lights from other passages, which are parallel or semi-parallel, and thus they educate their readers to compare spiritual things with spiritual. I would to God that we ministers kept closer to the grand old Book! We would be instructive preachers if we did, even if we were ignorant of "modern thought" and were not "abreast of the times." I guarantee you we would be leagues ahead of our times if we kept closer to the Word of God.

As for you who don't have to preach, the best food for you is the Word of God itself. *For the word of the LORD is right, and all his works are done in truth* (Psalm 33:4). Sermons and books are okay, but streams that run for a long distance above ground gradually gather some of the soil through which they flow, and they lose the cool freshness that they started with at the springhead. Truth is sweetest where it breaks from the smitten Rock, for at its first gush, it has lost none of its heavenliness and vitality. It is always best to drink at the well and not from the tank. You will find that reading the Word of God for yourselves, reading *it* rather than notes about it, is the surest way to grow in grace.

Much apparent Bible reading is not Bible reading at all. The verses pass under the eye, and the sentences glide over the mind, but there is no understanding. An old preacher used to say that the Word has mighty-free course among many these days, for it goes in at one of their ears and out at the other; so it seems to be with some readers – they can read a great deal, because they do not understand. The eye glances, but the mind never rests. The soul does not light upon the truth and stay there. It flits over the landscape as a bird might do, but it builds no nest there and finds no rest for its foot. Such reading is not reading. Understanding the meaning is the essence of true reading. Reading has a kernel to it, and the mere shell is worth little. In prayer, there is such a thing as praying in prayer. Likewise in praise, there is a praising in song, an inward fire of intense devotion that is the life of the hallelujah. Even

> **There must be knowledge of God before there can be love for God**

in fasting there is a fasting that is not fasting, and there is an inward fasting, a fasting of the soul, which is the soul of fasting. This also occurs with the reading of the Scriptures. There is an interior reading, a kernel reading – a true and living reading of the Word. This is the soul of reading, and if it isn't there, the reading is a mechanical exercise and profits nothing.

Certainly, the benefit of reading must come to the soul by the way of the understanding. *The exposition of thy words gives light; it gives understanding unto the simple* (Psalm 119:130). When the high priest went into the Holy Place, he always lit the golden candlestick before he kindled the incense upon the brazen altar, as if to show that the mind must have illumination before the affections can properly rise toward their divine object. There must be knowledge of God before there can be love for God; there must be knowledge of divine things, as they are revealed, before there can be an enjoyment of them. We must try to make out what God means by this and what He means by that; otherwise, we may kiss the Book and have no love for its contents; we may reverence the letter but have no devotion toward the Lord who speaks to us in these words. You will never get comfort for your soul from what you do not understand, nor find guidance for your life from what you do not comprehend. Nor can any practical influence upon your character come from what is not understood by you. *Through thy precepts I have obtained understanding; therefore I have hated every false way* (Psalm 119:104).

When we come to the study of Holy Scripture, we should try to have our mind alert to it. We are not always prepared to read the Bible. Sometimes we should stop before we open this volume. As God told Moses, *Put off thy shoes from thy feet; for the place where thou dost stand is holy ground* (Acts 7:33). If you have just come in from thought and anxiety about your worldly business, you cannot immediately take the Book and enter into its heavenly mysteries. As you ask a blessing over your meat before you eat, it would be a good rule for you to ask a blessing on the Word before you partake of its heavenly food. Pray to the Lord to strengthen your eyes before you dare look into the eternal light of Scripture. The priests washed their feet at the laver before they went to their holy work; so you should wash your soul's eyes before you look upon God's Word – wash even your fingers, the mental fingers that you use to turn from page to page. In this way you may deal with the Holy Book in a holy fashion.

Say to your soul, "Come, soul, wake up. You are

not about to read the newspaper; you are not perusing the pages of a human poet to be dazzled by his flashy poetry; you are coming near to God, who sits in the Word like a crowned monarch in his halls. Wake up, my glory; wake up all that is within me. Though I may not be praising and glorifying God now, I am about to consider what would lead me in this act of devotion. So, wake up, my soul, wake up, and don't fall asleep before the throne of the Eternal."

Scripture reading is our spiritual mealtime. Sound the gong and call in every ability to the Lord's own table to feast upon the precious meat that is now to be partaken of. Or rather, ring the church bell as for worship, for the studying of the Holy Scriptures should be as solemn a deed as when we worship on Sunday in the Lord's house.

To understand what you read, you will need to meditate upon it. Some passages of Scripture lie clear before us – blessed shallows in which the lambs can wade. But, there are depths in which our minds might drown rather than swim with pleasure, if we don't use caution. There are texts of Scripture which are made and constructed to make us think. By this means, among others, our heavenly Father educates us for heaven – by making us think our way into divine mysteries. Therefore, He puts the Word in a somewhat involved form to compel us to meditate upon it before we reach the sweetness. He might have explained it to us so we could catch the thought in a minute, but He doesn't want to do that in every case. Many of the veils which are cast over Scripture are not meant to hide the meaning from the diligent but to compel the mind to be active, for often the diligence of the heart in seeking to know the divine mind does the heart more good than the knowledge itself. Meditation and careful thought exercise us and strengthen the soul for the reception of the more glorious truths.

I heard that in times past the mothers in the Balearic Isles of the Mediterranean, who wanted their boys to be good slingers, would put their dinners up where they could not reach them until they threw a stone and fetched them down. Our Lord wishes us to be good slingers, and He places some precious truth in a lofty place where we cannot grasp it except by slinging at it or returning to it over and over. At last, we hit the mark and find food for our souls. Then we have the double benefit of learning the art of meditation and partaking of the sweet truth it has brought within our reach. We must meditate.

> These grapes will yield no wine until we tread upon them.

These grapes will yield no wine until we tread upon them. These olives must be put under the wheel and pressed again and again, so the oil can flow. In a dish of nuts, you know which nut has been eaten, because there is a little hole that an insect punctures through the shell, just a little hole, and inside there is the living thing eating up the kernel. Well, it is a grand thing to bore through the shell of the letter and then live inside feeding upon the kernel. I want to be such a little worm, living within and upon the Word of God after boring my way through the shell and reaching the innermost mystery of the blessed gospel. The Word of God is always most precious to the man who lives on it the most.

As I sat under a wide-spreading beech tree, I was pleased to notice the unique habits of that most wonderful tree, which seems to have an intelligence that other trees do not. I wondered at and admired the beech, but I thought to myself, I do not enjoy this beech tree half as much as that squirrel does. I see him leap from bough to bough, and I'm sure that he dearly values the old beech tree, because he has his home somewhere inside in a hollow place. These branches are his shelter, and those beechnuts are his food. He lives up in this tree. It is his world, his playground, his granary, his home; indeed, it is everything to him, and it is not so to me, for I find my rest and food elsewhere. With God's Word, we should be like squirrels, living in it and living on it. Let's exercise our minds and leap from bough to bough on it, find our rest and food in it, and make it everything to us. We shall be the people who profit from it if we make it our food, our medicine, our treasury, our armory, our rest, and our delight. May the Holy Spirit lead us to do this and make the Word precious to our souls.

Use all means and helps toward the understanding of the Scriptures. When Philip asked the Ethiopian eunuch whether he understood the prophecy of Isaiah, he replied, *How can I, except someone should guide me?* (Acts 8:31). Then Philip went up and opened the Word of the Lord for him. Some people refuse to be instructed by books or by living men under the pretense of being taught by the Spirit. This is not honoring the Spirit of

God; it is a disrespect to Him, for if He gives more light to some of His servants than to others – and it is clear He does – then they are bound to give that light to others and use it for the good of the church. But if the other part of the church refuses to receive that light, what use is the light that the Spirit of God gave? This would imply that there is a mistake somewhere in the dispensing of gifts and graces, which is managed by the Holy Spirit. It cannot be so.

The Lord Jesus Christ chooses to give more knowledge of His Word and more insight into it to some of His servants than to others, and it is ours to accept joyfully. It would be wicked of us to say, "We will not have the heavenly treasure which comes from earthen vessels. We will receive it if God will give it to us out of His own hand, but not through the earthen vessel. But we think we are too wise, too heavenly minded, too spiritual altogether to care for jewels when they are placed in earthen pots. We will not hear anybody, and we will not read anything except the Book itself; neither will we accept any light except that which comes through a crack in our own roof. We will not see by another man's candle; we would rather remain in the dark." Don't fall into such folly. Let the light come from God, and though a child shall bring it, we will joyfully accept it.

In reading, we ought to seek the spiritual teaching of the Word. Our Lord said, *Have ye not read?* Then again, *have ye not read?* and then He said, *If ye knew what this means,* and the meaning is very spiritual. The text he quoted was, *I will have mercy and not sacrifice*

(Matthew 12:3, 5, 7). This text came from the prophet Hosea: *For I desired mercy, and not sacrifice; and the knowledge of God more than burnt offerings* (Hosea 6:6). Now, the scribes and Pharisees were all for the letter of the law – the sacrifice, the killing of the bullock, and so on. They overlooked the spiritual meaning of the passage, *I will have mercy and not sacrifice* – namely, that God prefers that we should care for our fellow creatures rather than observe any ceremony of His law which caused hunger or thirst and death to any of the creatures that His hands had made. They should have passed beyond the outward into the spiritual, and all our readings should do the same.

This should be the case when we read the historical passages. *Have ye not read what David did, and those that were with him, when he was hungry, how he entered into the house of God and ate the showbread, which was not lawful for him to eat, neither for those who were with him, but only for the priests?* (Matthew 12:3-4). This was a piece of history, and they should have read it to find spiritual instruction in it.

I have sometimes found a greater depth of spirituality in the histories than I have even in the Psalms. When you reach the inner, spiritual meaning of a history, you are often surprised at the wondrous clearness and the realistic force with which the teaching comes to your soul. Some of the marvelous mysteries of revelation are better understood by being set in the histories than they are by the verbal declaration of them. When we have an explanation for the illustration, the illustration expands and brings the statement to life.

For instance, when our Lord explained what faith was, He reminded us of the brazen serpent. Who has ever read the story of the brazen serpent and not felt that he has a better understanding of faith through the picture of the dying, snake-bitten people who looked at the serpent of brass and lived? That was a stronger description than any that even Paul gave us, though he defined and described in a wondrous fashion.

The same thing is true with all the ceremonial precepts, because the Savior went on to say, *Have ye not read in the law, how that on the sabbath days the priests in the temple profane the sabbath and are blameless?* (Matthew 12:5). There is not a single precept in the old law that doesn't have an inner sense and meaning; therefore, don't turn away from Leviticus or say, "I cannot read these chapters in the books of Exodus and Numbers. They are all about the tribes and their standards, the stations in the wilderness and the halts of the march, the tabernacle and furniture, or about golden knops and bowls, and boards, and sockets, and precious stones, and blue and scarlet and fine linen." No, look for the inner meaning. Make a thorough search; in a king's treasure that is locked up the tightest and the hardest to reach is the choicest jewel of the treasure – so it is with the Holy Scriptures.

Did you ever go to the British Museum library? The reader is allowed to take down many reference books whenever he pleases, but he must write a ticket for other books, and he cannot get them without the ticket. Then they have certain choice books, which you will not see without a special order, without an unlocking of doors and opening of cases. A watcher is there with you while you make your inspection. You are scarcely allowed to put your eye on the manuscript for fear you might blot a letter out by glancing at it. Such a book is a precious treasure; there is not another copy of it in all the world, so you cannot get at it easily. Likewise, there are choice and precious doctrines of God's Word, which are locked up in cases like Leviticus or Solomon's Song, and you cannot get at them without unlocking doors; the

> The higher truths are as choicely hidden away as the precious regalia of princes; therefore, search as well as read.

Holy Spirit Himself must be with you, or you will never grasp the priceless treasure. The higher truths are as choicely hidden away as the precious regalia of princes; therefore, search as well as read. Don't be satisfied with a ceremonial precept until you reach its spiritual meaning, for that is true reading. You have not read until you understand the spirit of the matter.

You will get a thousand helps out of that wondrous Book if you just read it; by understanding the words more, you will prize it more. As you get older, the Book will grow with your growth and turn out to be an old man's manual of devotion just as it was a child's sweet storybook. Yes, it will always be a new Book – just as new a Bible as if it was printed yesterday and nobody had seen a word of it until now; yet it will be more precious for all the memories which cluster around it. As we turn its pages, we remember passages in our history which will never be forgotten for all eternity but will stand forever intertwined with gracious promises. The Lord taught us to read His Book of Life, which He has opened before us, so we might read our names in that other book of love that we have not seen yet, but which will be opened at the last great day.

Chapter 15

We Need Laborers

*Then he said unto his disciples, The harvest
truly is plenteous, but the labourers are few.*
– Matthew 9:37

Our Savior looked upon and moved among the
people in a manner worthy of our imitation. He
was a Man of great feeling: *And when he saw the multitude, he was moved with compassion on them because
they fainted and were scattered abroad, as sheep having no shepherd* (Matthew 9:36). His sympathies were
awakened; He could not look upon a mass of men with
an indifferent countenance. His inmost soul was stirred,
but at the same time, He was no mere enthusiast; He was
as calmly practical as if He had been a cool calculator.
He did something more than sigh; He proceeded to aid
those He pitied. He had practical compassion on the
crowd, so He turned to His disciples and said, *pray ye*

therefore the Lord of the harvest, that he will send forth labourers into his harvest (Matthew 9:38).

He did not go among the masses with an undiscerning admiration of them. I do not hear Him praising them as "the finest peasantry" or "the sinew of the nation," as some will do, but neither do we see in Him any trace of aversion to them, as though He felt out of place in their society. He was often saddened by their foolishness and grieved by their sins, but He never loathed them or spoke contemptuously of them. The common people heard Him gladly, because they saw that He had sympathy for them. Though in character grandly aristocratic, He was in manner and life profoundly common and compassionate; He was a King, and yet *one chosen out of* [the] *people*, who loved them with all His heart (Psalm 89:19). It is clear that He never grew discouraged in laboring for their good; you never hear Him say that it is useless to preach to the multitude, that they are too degraded, too priest-ridden, or too ignorant. No discouragement ever dampened His passion; He persevered until His work was done. Jesus possessed a brave and glorious heart that always melted to tenderness but at the same time was always practical. He was never influenced by admiration, or aversion, or discouragement in a way that He'd cease from practical methods of bettering the condition of the people among whom He dwelt.

He persevered until His work was done.

The thought of the multitude rises from the sight of a harvest field. When the crop is plenteous, the idea of a multitude forces itself upon you at once. You cannot count the ears of corn; neither will you be able to count the sons of men. I suppose our Savior alluded to the crowds around Himself first, but His mind was more extensive than ours. He remembered all the thousands of Israel. He could not have restricted His heart to the little country of Israel. He glanced across the seas and beyond the mountains to the myriads of mankind swarming upon this globe.

It crushes one to think of the millions of humans. It is difficult to obtain an idea of the vast extent of our huge city; you could travel from one end to the other as long as you want and study its statistics, but you can't truly comprehend what the population is. But what is one city compared to our nation and with the millions that speak our language all over the world? Yet even these are just a small portion of the innumerable host. We shall never be able to comprehend a nation like China with its teeming millions or northern India. Multitudes are in the valley of existence, as the drops from the rain cloud and as the leaves upon the forest trees – such are the sons of men.

But when the Lord spoke of them as a harvest, He realized the danger to them. Suppose the owner of some large estate walked through his acres and said, "I have a great harvest – look at those far-reaching fields. But the country has become depopulated, the people have emigrated, and I have no laborers. There are one or two over there, and they are reaping with all their might. They work long days and labor until they faint, but over here there are vast acres of my farm not reaped, and I don't have a sickle to thrust in. The corn is being wasted, and it grieves me. See how the birds gather in flocks to prey upon the precious ears! Meanwhile, the season is far advanced, and the autumn dampness is already upon us. The chilly, frosty nights, which are winter's forefront, are on their way. Mildew is spoiling the grain, and what remains will shell out on the ground or swell with the moisture and become useless."

Imagine the Redeemer in this picture. He looks at the world today, and He says, "All these multitudes of precious souls will be lost, for there are so few reapers to gather them in. Here and there are men who, with immense energy, are reaping all they can and are all but fainting as they reap; I am with them, and blessed sheaves are taken home, but what are these among so many?" Look, can your eye see it? Can even an eagle's wing fly over the vast fields without growing weary in the flight? There are the precious ears – they decay, they rot, they perish, they are ruined. They are lost to God and to their own eternal injury; it grieves the Great Husbandman that it is so. That is still the case today, and it should grieve us that it is this way, for His sake and for the sake of our fellow men.

The Savior had yet another thought, namely, that the masses were accessible, for He used the same expression when the people came streaming out of Samaria to the well to hear Him. They were drawn by curiosity created by the woman's story. He said to His disciples, *Lift up your eyes and look on the fields, for they are white already to harvest* (John 4:35). When people are ready to hear the Word, the fields are ripe. Our Lord explained that as the wheat ears do not oppose the sickle but stand there, waiting for a man to enter the field and use the sickle, the result will surely follow. Likewise, there are times when nothing is lacking except to preach the gospel, and the souls that otherwise would perish will surely be gathered.

Who have gathered the crowds? Such men as Augustine and Chrysostom.[12] And what was their preaching other than the gospel of Jesus Christ? Who joined them? Such men as John Huss, and Jerome, and Luther, and Calvin who were a sweet savor of Christ.[13] Who joined them in this land? Who but our Wycliffe and our Knox?[14]

> There are times when nothing is lacking except to preach the gospel.

Who joined them in later days but our George Whitefield and John Wesley, men who spoke the common language of the people and had no theme but Jesus crucified. People will not come out to hear your philosophies; they leave you and your philosophies to the spiders and the dry rot, but if you preach Jesus and His precious blood and tell men that whoever believes in Christ shall be saved, those people will hear you gladly.

---

12 Augustine (354-430) was a fourth-century philosopher, known for writing *Confessions*, his autobiographical work outlining his sinful youth and conversion to Christianity. John Chrysostom (347-407) was considered one of the best preachers in the early church and a leading intellectual.

13 John Huss (1369-1415) outlined his case for reform of the church and was burned at the stake. Jerome (347-420) was a theologian and historian.

14 John Wycliffe (1320-1384) was an English Protestant theologian and church reformer best known for translating the Bible into the common language. John Knox (ca. 1513-1572) was a Scottish minister and theologian who was a leader in the Reformation.

I heard from a missionary who spends nights working for his Lord in gin palaces and the lowest resorts of the people, that he was rarely met with an insult. The people received his tracts and thanked him for his kind words. Our city missionaries and those who visit taxicab stands or bus stations or work among other public servants say that, in general, there is a willing attention to the gospel. The fields stand asking us to reap them, but there are not enough reapers; the grain perishes for want of laborers. The people are accessible. What country is there where the gospel cannot be preached? China was closed fast, but now you can go throughout the length and breadth of the land and talk of Christ, if you want to. Japan is open to you, and Africa has laid her central secret bare. Spain, shut tight as with a seal, is set free today, and Italy rejoices in the same liberty. The whole world lies before the reapers of the Most High, but where are the reapers? *The harvest truly is plenteous, but the labourers are few.*

The idea of immediate need is contained in this figure of speech, for the reaping of the harvest is a matter of now or never to the farmer. "Ah," says he, "if I could postpone the harvest and let it be gathered in by slow degrees, if we could work until the harvest moon has gone and then through November and December until winter comes, then the few number of laborers would be a small problem. But there is a limited time in which the wheat can be safely brought in, and it must be before winter begins, or it is lost to us." There is no time for us to waste in the salvation of the sons of men. They will not live forever; older men will not wait until you have told them the gospel, if you postpone the good news for the next ten years. We speak of what we hope may be accomplished for our race in half a century, but this generation will be buried before that time. You must reap the harvest at once, or it will be destroyed; it must be gathered speedily, or it will perish. Today, today, today – the imperative necessities of manhood appeal to the benevolence of Christians. Today, the sure destruction of the unbeliever speaks with pleading voice to the humanity of every quickened heart: "We are perishing; will you let us perish? You can only help us by bringing us the gospel now; will you delay?"

Chapter 16

Save the Children

And he said unto them, Follow me, and will make you fishers of men. – Matthew 4:19

I hope you do not neglect Sunday school, but I am afraid many Christians are scarcely aware that there are such things as Sunday schools at all. They have heard of it in conversations but not by observation. Probably in the course of twenty years, they have never visited a Sunday school or concerned themselves about it. They would be pleased to hear of any success accomplished, but though they may not have heard anything about the matter one way or the other, they are content. In most churches you will find a group of young, passionate spirits giving themselves to Sunday school work, but there are many others who could strengthen the school but never attempt anything of the sort. In this they might be excused if they had other work to do, but unfortunately, they have no godly occupation. They are mere killers of time, while this work lies ready to do, is accessible, and demands their assistance but is entirely neglected. I will not say there are any such sluggards here, but I can't believe that we are free of them. Therefore, I will ask consciences to do their work with the guilty parties.

Children need to be saved; children can be saved; children are to be saved by an intermediary. Children can be saved while they are children. He who said, *Suffer the little children to come unto me and forbid them not, for of such is the kingdom of the heavens* never intended that His church should say, "We will look after the children by and by when they have grown up to be young men and women" (Matthew 19:14). He intended that children should be a subject of prayer, and with earnest effort they should be converted to God as children. The conversion of a child involves the same work of divine grace and results in the same blessed consequences as the conversion of an adult. One such consequence is saving the soul of the child from death and hiding a multitude of sins, but there is an additional matter for joy. A great preventive work is done when the young are converted. Conversion saves a child from a multitude of sins. If God's eternal mercy blesses your teaching of a little jabberbox, how happy that boy's life will be compared to what might have been if he had grown up in foolishness, sin, and shame.

It is the highest wisdom and best judgment to pray for our children that while they are young their hearts may be given to the Savior. To reclaim the prodigal is a good thing, but to save him from ever becoming a prodigal is better. To bring back the thief and the drunkard is a praiseworthy action, but to influence the boy so he never becomes a thief or a drunkard is far better. Therefore, Sunday school instruction stands very high in the list of philanthropic enterprises, and Christians should be earnest about it. He who converts a child from the error of the world prevents as well as covers a multitude of sins, for we know that *whosoever causes the sinner to convert from the error of his way shall save a soul from death and shall cover a multitude of sins* (James 5:20).

Moreover, the church acquires the hope of being furnished with the best men and women. The church's Samuels and Solomons are made wise in their youth; Davids and Josiahs were tender of heart when they were tender in years. Read about the most esteemed ministers, and you will usually find that their Christian history began early. Though it is not mandatory, it is highly advantageous to the growth of a well-developed Christian character for its foundation to be grounded on youthful devotion. I do not expect to see the churches of Jesus Christ ordinarily built up by those who have lived in sin throughout their lives, but by those young men and women who have been brought up in the fear and admonition of the Lord; they are the ones who become pillars in the house of our God. If we want strong Christians, we must look to those who were Christians in their youth;

> He who converts a child from the error of the world prevents as well as covers a multitude of sins.

trees must be planted in the courts of the Lord while still young if they are to flourish.

The work of teaching the young is more important than it has ever been before, for at this time there are those around the world who are creeping into our houses and deluding men and women with their false doctrine. Let the Sunday schools teach the children well. Let them not merely occupy their time with pious phrases, but let them teach them the whole gospel and the doctrines of grace intelligently; let them pray over the children and never be satisfied unless the children are turned to the Lord Jesus Christ and added to the church. We have laid aside catechisms sometimes with too little reason, but if we do not use godly catechisms, we must bring back decided, plain, simple teaching, and there must be pleading and praying for the conversion of the children, the immediate conversion of children to the Lord Jesus Christ. The Spirit of God waits to help us in this effort. *The Comforter, which is the Holy Spirit, whom the Father will send in my name, he shall teach you all things and bring to your remembrance all the things that I have said unto you* (John 14:26). He is with us if we are with Him. He is ready to bless the humblest teacher, and even the infant classes will not be without a blessing. He can give us words and thoughts suitable to our little ones. He can so bless us that we will know how to speak a word in season to the youthful ear. But if teachers are not found or are not faithful, we will see the children who have been in our schools go back into the world. Like their parents, they will hate religion because of the tedious hours spent in the

Sunday school, and we will produce a race of infidels or a generation of superstitious persons. The golden opportunity will be lost, and the blame will rest on us. I pray for the church of God to value the Sunday school. I plead for all who love the nation to pray for Sunday schools. I entreat all who love Jesus Christ and want to see His kingdom come to be tender toward all young people and pray that their hearts may be won to Jesus.

The theme lies very near to my heart, and it should press heavily on all our consciences. God must lead your thoughts into it; I leave it, but not until I have asked these questions: What have each one of you been doing for the conversion of children? What have you done for the conversion of your own children? Are you quite clear about this matter? Do you ever put your arms around your boy's neck and pray for him and with him? Father, you will find that such an act will exercise great influence over your boy. Mother, do you ever talk to your little daughter about Christ and Him crucified? Under God's hands, you may be a spiritual as well as a natural mother to that beloved child of yours. What are you doing, you who are guardians and teachers of youth? Are you clear about their souls? Do all of you teachers, both weekday and Sunday, do all you should so your boys and girls may be brought to confess the Lord at an early age? I leave it with you. You shall receive a great reward if, when you enter heaven, you find many dear children there to

> Under God's hands, you may be a spiritual as well as a natural mother to that beloved child of yours.

welcome you into eternal life. It will add another heaven to your own heaven to meet with heavenly beings who salute you as their teacher who brought them to Jesus. I would not wish to go to heaven alone – would you? I don't want to have a crown in heaven without a star on it because of my failure to teach and lead a child to Jesus – do you?

Imagine: there they go – the sacred flock of blood-bought sheep, and the great Shepherd leads them; many of them are followed by twins, and others have their lambs. Would you like to be a barren sheep of the great Shepherd's flock? The scene changes. Hearken to the trampings of a great host. I hear their war music, and my ears are filled with their songs of victory. The warriors are coming home, and each one is bringing his trophy on his shoulder to the honor of the great Captain. They stream through the gates of pearl; they march in triumph to the celestial Capitol along the golden streets, and each soldier bears with him his own portion of the spoil. Will you be there? And if you are, will you march without a trophy and add nothing to the pomp of the triumph? Will you bear nothing that you won in battle, nothing that you have taken for Jesus with your sword and with your bow?

Again, another scene is before me: I hear them shout the "harvest home" and see the reapers each bearing his sheaf. Some of them are bowed down with the heaps of sheaves which load the happy shoulders. These went out weeping, but they rejoice as they return and bring the sheaves with them. Here comes one who only brings a little handful, but it is rich grain; he only had a tiny plot and a little seed corn entrusted to him, and it has multiplied well according to the rule of proportion. Will you be there without even a solitary ear, because you never plowed or sowed and therefore never reaped? If so, every shout of every reaper might well strike a fresh pang into your heart as you remember that you did not sow and therefore could not reap. If you do not love my Master, do not profess to do so. If He never bought you with His blood, do not lie to Him, or come to His table, and say that you are His servant. But if His wounds bought you, give yourself to Him. If you love Him, feed His sheep and feed His lambs. He stands here unseen by my sight but recognized by my faith. He exhibits the marks of the wounds upon His hands and His feet, and He says to you, *Peace be unto you; as my Father has sent me, even so send I you. Go ye into all the world and preach the gospel to every creature*; remember *that whosoever causes the sinner to convert from the error of his way shall save a soul from death and shall cover a multitude of sins* (John 20:21; Mark 16:15; James 5:20).

Chapter 17

Saving a Soul

Restore unto me the joy of thy saving health,
and thy spirit of liberty shall uphold me.
Then I will teach transgressors thy ways,
and sinners shall be converted unto thee.
– Psalm 51:12-13

If anyone has been the means of restoring a back-slider, it is said, *Let him know* (James 5:20 KJV). That is, let him think about it and be sure of it; let him be comforted by it and inspired by it. *Let him know* it and never doubt it. Do not merely hear it, but let it sink deep into your heart. When an apostle, inspired by the Holy Spirit, says, *Let him know*, do not let any laziness of spirit forbid your determining the full weight of the truth. What is it that you are to know? You are to know that he who converts a sinner from the error of his way shall save a soul from death. This is something worth knowing; it is no small matter. We have men among us whom we honor every time we cast our eyes upon them, for they have saved many precious lives. They have manned the lifeboat, or they have plunged into the river to rescue the drowning. They have been ready to risk their own lives amidst burning timbers so they might snatch the perishing from the devouring flames.

True heroes these men are and far worthier of honor than your bloodstained men of war. God bless the brave hearts! May our country never lack a body of worthy men to make her shores famous for humanity. When we see a fellow creature exposed to danger, our heart beats quickly, and we are agitated with a desire to save him. Isn't it so? But the saving of a soul from death is a far greater matter. Let us think what that death is! It is not nonexistence; I do not know that I would lift a finger to save my fellow creature from mere nonexistence. I see no great hurt in annihilation – certainly nothing that would alarm me as a punishment for sin, just as I see no great joy in mere eternal existence, if that is all that is meant by eternal life. I discern no terror in ceasing to be; I would as soon not be as be, as far as mere colorless being or not being is concerned. But eternal life in Scripture is a very different thing from eternal existence; it means existing with all the faculties developed in fullness of joy – existing not as the dried herb in the hay but as the flower in all its beauty. To die in Scripture is not ceasing to exist. The difference between the words *to die* and *to be annihilated* is enormous. To die the first death is the separation of the body from the soul; it is the dividing of our nature into its component elements. To die the second death is to separate the man, soul, and body from his God, who is the life and joy of our manhood. This is eternal destruction from the presence of the Lord and from the glory of His power. This is to have the palace of manhood destroyed and turned into a desolate ruin for the howling dragon of remorse and the hooting owl of despair to inherit forever.

Remember, your Savior came to this world with two objectives: He came to destroy death and to put away sin. If you convert a sinner from the error of his ways, you are like Him in both these works. In the power of the Spirit of God, you overcome death by snatching a soul from the second death, and you put away sin from the sight of God by hiding a multitude of sins beneath the propitiation of the Lord Jesus.

> The apostle does not say if you convert a sinner from the error of his ways you will have honor.

The apostle does not say if you convert a sinner from the error of his ways you will have honor. True philanthropy scorns such a motive. He does not say if you convert a sinner from the error of his ways you will have the respect of the church and the love of the individual. Such will be the case, but we are moved by nobler motives. The joy of doing good is found in the good itself; the reward of a deed of love is found in its own result. If we have saved a soul from death and hidden a multitude of sins, that is payment enough, even if no ear should ever hear of the deed, and no pen should ever record it. Let it be forgotten that we were the instrument if good has been effected. It will give us joy even if we are not appreciated and are left in the cold shade of forgetfulness. Even if others claim the honors of the good deed that the Lord has accomplished by us, we will not murmur; it will be joy enough to know that a soul has been saved from death, and a multitude of sins have been covered.

Let's remember that the saving of souls from death honors Jesus, for there is no saving of souls except through His blood. As for you and me, what can we do in saving a soul from death? By ourselves nothing, any more than that pen which lies upon the table could write *The Pilgrim's Progress*, but let a Bunyan grasp the pen, and the matchless work is written. So you and I can do nothing to convert souls until God's eternal Spirit takes us in hand, but then He can do wonders by us and get the glory by us, while it will be joy enough for us to know that Jesus is honored and the Spirit magnified. Nobody talks of Homer's pen; no one has encased it in gold or published its illustrious achievements. Nor do we wish for honor among men; it will be enough for us to have been the pen in the Savior's hand with which He has written the covenant of His grace upon the fleshy tablets of human hearts. These are golden wages for a man who loves his Master; Jesus is glorified, and sinners are saved.

The apostle says all that about the conversion of one person. *If any of you have erred from the truth, and someone should convert him; let that one know, that whosoever causes the sinner to convert from the error of his way shall save a soul from death* (James 5:19-20). Have you never wished you were a Whitefield? Have you never felt in your inmost soul great aspirations to be another McCheyne, or Brainerd, or Moffat?[15] Cultivate the aspiration, but at the same time be happy to bring one sinner to Jesus Christ, for he who converts one has saved a soul from death and covered a multitude of sins.

Scripture does not say anything about the person who achieved this work. It does not say, "If a minister shall convert a man, or if some eloquent holy person shall have wrought it." If this deed is performed by the youngest child or a child tells the story of Jesus to his father, that child will have saved a soul. If a servant girl drops a tract where some poor soul finds it and receives salvation, she will have saved a soul from death. If the humblest preacher on the street corner speaks to the thief or to the harlot, and that one is saved, he will have turned a sinner from the error of his ways, saved a soul from death, and covered a multitude of sins.

May we long to be used in the conversion of sinners. James does not speak about the Holy Spirit in this passage nor of the Lord Jesus Christ, for he was writing to those who remembered the important truths about both the Spirit and the Son of God. However, we cannot do spiritual good to our fellow man apart from the Spirit of God; neither can we be a blessing to them if we do not preach to them *Jesus Christ and him crucified* (1 Corinthians 2:2). God must use us; let us pray and long to be used; let us purge ourselves of everything

---

15 Robert McCheyne (1813-1854) was a Presbyterian minister and missionary who designed a plan to read through the Bible in a year. David Brainerd (1718-1747) was an American missionary to the Native Americans. Robert Moffat (1795-1883) was a Scottish Congregationalist missionary to Africa.

that would prevent our being employed by the Lord. If there is anything we are doing or leaving undone, any evil we are harboring or any grace we are neglecting, which may make us unfit to be used of God, let us pray the Lord to cleanse, and mend, and scour us until we are vessels fit for the Master's use. Then let us be on the watch for opportunities of usefulness; let us go about the world with our ears and eyes open, ready to offer ourselves in every occasion for doing good; let us not be content until we are useful, but make this the main design and ambition of our lives.

> *But in a great house there are not only vessels of gold and of silver, but also of wood and of clay, and likewise some to honour, and some to dishonor. If a man, therefore, purges himself from these things, he shall be a vessel unto honour, sanctified, and profitable for the master's use, and prepared unto every good work.* (2 Timothy 2:20-21)

Chapter 18

Restoring Those
Who Have Erred

Brethren, if any of you have erred from the
truth, and someone should convert him; let
that one know, that whosoever causes the
sinner to convert from the error of his way
shall save a soul from death and shall cover
a multitude of sins. – James 5:19-20

James is supremely practical. If he is the James who
was called the Just, I can understand how he earned
the title, for that distinguishing trait in his character
shows itself in his epistle. If he is the Lord's brother,
he did well to resemble so closely his great relative and
Master, who started His ministry with the practical
Sermon on the Mount. We should be grateful that
in the Holy Scriptures we have food for all classes of
believers and employment for all the skills of the saints.

It was appropriate that the thoughtful should be

furnished with abundant subjects for pondering. Paul has supplied them; he has given us sound doctrine, arranged in the symmetry of exact order. He has given us deep thoughts and profound teachings; he has opened up the deep things of God. No man who is inclined to reflection and thoughtfulness will be without food as long as the epistles of Paul exist, for he feeds the soul with sacred manna.

For those who are inclined to more supernatural themes, John has written sentences glowing with devotion and blazing with love. We have his simple but sublime epistles – epistles that seem to be fit for children, but when examined, their core substance seems too sublime to be fully grasped by the most advanced of men. That same eagle-eyed and eagle-winged apostle gave us the wondrous vision of the Revelation, where awe, devotion, and imagination increase and find scope for the fullest exercise.

One class of people, however, are more practical than contemplative and more active than imaginative. It was wise that there should be a James, whose main point would stir up their remembrance and help them persevere in the practical graces of the Holy Spirit.

Here is a special case of a backslider from the church: *if any of you* refers to a professed Christian. The erring one had been named by the name of Jesus and for a while had followed the truth, but in an evil hour he had been deceived into doctrinal error and had strayed from the truth. He did not merely fall into a mistake in some lesser matter, which might be compared to the fringe of the gospel, but he erred in some vital doctrine

– he departed from the faith in its fundamentals. Some truths must be believed; they are essential to salvation, and if not heartily accepted, the soul will be ruined. This man had been professedly orthodox, but he turned aside from the truth on an essential point.

Now, in those days the saints did not say, "We must be tender and loving and leave this brother to his own opinion; he sees truth from a different perspective and has a rather different way of putting it, but his opinions are as good as our own, and we must not say that he is in error." That is the fashionable way of trifling with divine truth and making things pleasant all around. Thus, the gospel is debased and another gospel propagated. I would like to ask modern churchmen if any doctrine would be worth a man burning at the stake or lying in prison. I do not believe they could give me an answer, for if their liberal philosophy is correct, the martyrs were fools of the first magnitude. From their writings and teachings, it appears that the modern thinkers treat all revealed truth with entire indifference. Even though they may feel sorry that wilder individuals go too far in free thinking, and they'd rather they would be more moderate, their liberality is so encompassing that they are not sure enough of anything to be able to condemn any transgression as a deadly error. To them, black and white are terms which may be applied to the same color as you view it from different standpoints. *Yea* and *nay* are equally true in their esteem. Their theology shifts like the Goodwin Sands, and they regard all firmness as much bigotry.[16] Errors and truths are equally comprehensible within the circle of their charity.

The apostles did not regard error in this way. They did not prescribe large-hearted charity towards falsehood or hold up the spiritual offender as a man of deep thought, whose views were "refreshingly original." They never uttered some wicked nonsense about the probability of their having more faith in honest doubt than in half the creeds. They did not believe in justification by doubting, as our cynics do. The apostles set about the conversion of the erring brother; they treated him as a person who needed conversion and viewed him as a man who would suffer the death of his soul if he were not converted. They were not easygoing people like our cultured friends of the school of "modern thought."

These modern thinkers have learned that the deity of Christ may be denied, the work of the Holy Spirit ignored, the inspiration of Scripture rejected, the atonement disbelieved, and regeneration dispensed with. They hold that the man who does all this may be as good a Christian as the most devout believer! O God, deliver us from this deceitful infidelity. It does damage to the erring man and often prevents his being restored. It even does mischief to our own hearts by teaching us that truth is not important, and falsehood a trifle; in this way it destroys our allegiance to the God of truth

---

16 Goodwin Sands is a treacherous stretch of sand in Britain along the English Channel. Because of the tides and currents, the sands are constantly shifting.

and makes us traitors instead of loyal subjects to the King of Kings.

It appears that this man followed the natural, logical consequence of doctrinal error and erred in his life as well, for the twentieth verse, which must be read in connection with the nineteenth, speaks of him as a sinner converted *from the error of his way*. His way went wrong after his thought had gone wrong. You cannot deviate from truth without, in some measure, deviating from practical righteousness. This man had erred from right acting because he had erred from right believing. Suppose a man accepts a doctrine that leads him to think little of Christ; he will soon have little faith in Him and become less obedient to Him. He will wander into self-righteousness or licentiousness. If a man thinks lightly of the punishment of sin, it is natural that he will commit sin with less conscience and will burst through all restraints. If he denies the need of atonement, the same result will follow as he acts out his belief in modern philosophy. Every error has its own outgrowth, as all decay has its appropriate fungus. It is in vain for us to imagine that holiness will be as readily produced from error as from truthful doctrine. Do men gather grapes from thorns or figs from thistles? The facts of history prove the contrary. When truth is dominant, morality and holiness are abundant; but when error comes to the front, godly living retreats in shame.

The point directed to this sinner in thought and deed was his conversion – turning him around and bringing him to right thinking and right acting. Alas!

I fear many do not look upon backsliders in this light; neither do they regard them as hopeful subjects for conversion. I know a person who had erred, but he was hunted down like a wolf. He was wrong to some degree, but that wrong had been aggravated until the man was worried into defiance. The fault was exaggerated into a double wrong by ferocious attacks upon him. His manhood took sides with his error because he had been so severely treated. The man was sinfully compelled to take up an extreme position and go further into mischief, because he could not bear to be denounced instead of being reasoned with.

And when a man has been blameworthy in his life, his fault will often be blazed abroad, retold from mouth to mouth, and magnified, until the poor erring man feels degraded. Having lost all self-respect, he gives way to more dreadful sins. The objective of some professors seems to be to amputate the limb rather than to heal it. Justice reigns instead of mercy. They tend to say, "Away with him! He is too foul to be washed, too diseased to be restored."

This is not according to the mind of Christ, nor after the model of apostolic churches. In the days of James, if any man erred from the truth and from holiness, some brethren sought his recovery and found joy in saving a soul from death. There is something very significant in that expression, *Brethren, if any of you have erred from the truth.* It is akin to that other word, *Considering thyself lest thou also be tempted*, and that other exhortation, *Let him that thinks he stands take heed lest he fall* (James 5:19; Galatians 6:1; 1 Corinthians 10:12). He who has erred was one of you, one who sat with you at the communion table, one with whom you took sweet counsel. He has been deceived, and by the subtlety of Satan he has been lured, but do not judge him harshly; above all, do not allow him to perish without mercy. If he ever was a saved man, he is still your brother, and it is your business to bring back the prodigal and make your Father's heart glad. In spite of all his slips, he is one of God's children; follow up with him and do not rest until you lead him home again.

If he is not a child of God and his professed conversion was a mistake, or a pretense, or if he only made a profession but had not the possession of vital godliness, approach him with sacred love, remembering how terrible his doom will be for daring to play the hypocrite and profaning holy things with his unhallowed hands. Weep over him if you feel compelled to suspect that he has been a willful deceiver, for there is sevenfold cause for weeping. If you cannot resist the feeling that he never was sincere but crept into the church under cover of a false profession, sorrow over him, for his doom will be more terrible. *If any of you have erred from the truth, and someone should convert him.* Who? The minister? No, any one among the brethren. If the minister is the means of the restoration of a backslider, he is a happy man, and a good deed has been done. But there is nothing said here concerning preachers or pastors; not even a hint is given. This work is left open to any one member of the church, and the plain inference is that every church member seeing his brother err from the truth, or err in practice, should set himself in the power of the Holy Spirit to this business of converting this special sinner from the error of his ways. Look after strangers, but don't neglect your brothers. It is the business, not of certain officers appointed by the church, but of every member of the body of Jesus Christ, to seek the good of all the other members.

There are certain members upon whom this may be more imperative. For instance, in the case of a young believer, if his father and his mother are believers, they are called upon by a sevenfold obligation to seek the conversion of their backsliding child. In the case of a husband, none should be as earnest for his restoration as his wife, and the same rule holds with regard to the wife for her husband. If the connection is that of friendship, whomever you have had the closest relationship with

When you perceive that he has gone astray, you should act the shepherd towards him with kindhearted zeal.

should lie nearest to your heart, and when you perceive that he has gone astray, you should act the shepherd towards him with kindhearted zeal. You are bound to do this with all your fellow Christians, but doubly bound to those over whom you possess an influence which has been nurtured by former intimacy, relationship, or any other means. I urge you, therefore, to watch over one another in the Lord, and when you see a brother *overtaken in a fault, ye who are spiritual restore such a one in the spirit of meekness* (Galatians 6:1). You see your duty; do not neglect it.

It should cheer us to know that the attempt to

convert a man who has erred from the truth is a hopeful one; success can be anticipated, and when the success comes, it will be of the most joyful character. Truly, it is a great joy to capture the wild, wandering sinner, but the joy of joys is to find the lost sheep that was once in the fold and had sadly gone astray. It is a great thing to transform a piece of brass into silver, but to the poor woman it was joy enough to find the lost piece of silver which was silver already and had the king's stamp on it. To bring in a stranger and an alien and adopt him as a son suggests a festival, but the most joyous feasting and the loudest music are for the son who was always a son but had played the prodigal; after being lost, he was found, and after being dead, he was made alive again. I say, ring the bells twice for the restored backslider; ring them until the steeple rocks and reels. Rejoice doubly over that which had gone astray and was ready to perish but has now been restored.

Consider Peter, who had denied his Master and wept bitterly when he realized what he had done. He was distraught, until the Lord Himself said, *Simon, son of Jonas, lovest thou me?* (John 21:15). The return of a backslider is no small matter even in comparison to restoring a harlot or a drunkard, but in the sight of God, it is a miracle of grace. Seek those who have gone from us; seek those who linger in the congregation but have disgraced the church and are put away from us because we cannot tolerate their uncleanness; seek them with prayers, and tears, and entreaties, if possibly God may grant them repentance that they may be saved.

Chapter 19

The Weeping Sower

He that goes forth and weeps, bearing the precious seed, shall doubtless come again with rejoicing, bringing his sheaves with him. – Psalm 126:6

A nd weeps. What does this word *weeps* mean? As in the first words, *he that goes forth*, we see the man's service, so here we note a little of the man himself. He *goes forth and weeps*. The man likely to be successful is a man of like passions with ourselves, not an angel, but a man, for he weeps. But he is very much a man; he is a man of strong passions, weeping because he has a sensitive heart. The man who sleeps and can be content to do nothing and is satisfied with no result is not the man to win souls. God usually chooses men, not of great intelligence and vast comprehension, but men of truehearted, deep natures, with souls that desire, and pant, and long, and heave, and throb for the lost. It is a great thing that makes a genuine man weep. Tears do not lie with most of us; but the man who cannot weep cannot preach. If he never feels tears within, even if they do not show themselves on the outside, he can scarcely be the man to handle such themes as those which God has committed to His people's charge.

If you want to be useful, you must cultivate the sacred passions. You must meditate on the divine realities until they move and stir your souls. You must consider that men are dying, Christ is dishonored, souls are not converted, the Holy Spirit is grieved, and the kingdom does not come to God, but Satan rules and reigns. Our hearts should be stirred like the prophet, and we can say, *Oh that my head were waters and my eyes a fountain of tears* (Jeremiah 9:1). The useful worker for Christ is a man of tenderness, not a stoic. He is not one who does not care whether souls are saved or not or is so wrapped up in the thought of divine sovereignty that he is absolutely petrified. He is one who feels as if he died in the death of sinners and perished in their ruin, as though he could only be made happy in their happiness or find a paradise in their being caught up to heaven.

The weeping shows you what kind of man the Lord of the harvest largely employs. He is a man in earnest, a man of tenderness, a man in love with souls, a man wrapped up in his calling, a man carried away with compassion, and a man who feels for sinners. In a word, he is a Christlike man, not a stone, but a man who is touched with a feeling of our infirmities, a man of heart, a man ready to weep because sinners will not weep. "Why does he weep?" someone asks. "He is doing honorable work, and he should have a glorious reward!"

He weeps as he goes forth because he feels his own insufficiency. He did not know what a weak creature he was until he came into contact with other men's hearts. He often sighs within himself, "Who is sufficient for these things?" He thought it was easy work to serve God, but now he is somewhat of Joshua's mind: *Ye cannot serve the LORD* (Joshua 24:19). Every effort that he makes exposes to him his own lack of natural strength. Yes, he may weep. He never teaches in the Sunday school class, and he never prays at the

Moreover, he weeps because of the hardness of men's hearts.

sick bed, but he feels ashamed when he has done his work because he did not do it better. He never takes a little child on his knee to talk to him about Jesus, but he wishes that he could have spoken more tenderly of the sweet gentleness of the Lover of little children. He is never satisfied with himself, for he forms a correct estimate of himself, and he weeps to think that he is so poor an instrument for so good a Master.

Moreover, he weeps because of the hardness of men's hearts. At first, he thought he should only have to tell these great truths and men would leap for joy. Have you ever seen fancy pictures on our missionary magazines of respectable gentlemen dressed in black suits? They come ashore with Bibles in their hands from boats manned by devout sailors. These well-to-do evangelists are surrounded by Turks and Chinese, black people and copper-colored people, who are running down to the seashore and taking these precious Bibles, looking as if they had found a priceless treasure. Ah, it is all in the picture, it is nowhere else. This does not occur in real life; natives of barbarous isles and heathen kingdoms do not receive the gospel in that way. Ambassadors of the cross have to do a great deal of rough work and have to toil on, for the gospel, which ought to be welcomed, is rejected. As there was no room for Christ in the inn when He became incarnate, so there is no room for the gospel in the hearts of mankind. Yes, and this makes us weep, because where there should be so much readiness to accept it, there is so much obstinacy and rebellion.

The Christian worker weeps, because when he does see some signs of success, he is often disappointed. Blossoms don't come to be fruit, or half-ripe fruit drops from the tree. He often has to weep before God, because he is afraid that these failures may be the result of his own lack of tact or grace. I don't marvel that any worker for Christ sprinkles the seed with his tears; the wonder is that he does not lament far more than he does. Perhaps we would all weep more if we were more Christlike – more of what we should be. Perhaps our work would have more blessed results if it came more from our very soul or if we played less at soul saving and worked more at it. If we cast soul and strength and every bit of energy of our being into the work, maybe God would reward us at a far greater rate.

Bearing the precious seed. Workers for God must tell the gospel and keep to the gospel. You must continually dwell upon the real truth, as it is in God's Word, for nothing but this will win souls. Now, in order to do this, workers for Christ must know God's truth. We must know it by an inward experience of its power as well as in the theory. We must know it as a precious truth. It must be precious seed to us, for which we should be prepared to die if it were necessary. We must understand it as being precious because it comes from God, precious because it tells man the best of news, precious because it is sprinkled with the blood of Jesus, and precious because Christ values it, and all holy men esteem it beyond all price. We must not deliver it with flippancy or talk of solemn themes with levity. We should not share the gospel as though we were relating a mere tale from *The Arabian Nights*, a romance meant for amusement, or entertainment to pass time. We who sow for God must sow in earnest, because the seed is more precious than we can ever estimate.

Work for God as those who know that the truth is a seed. Do not speak of it and forget it. Do not tell the gospel as though it were a stone and will lie on the ground and never spring up. Share the truth with the firm conviction that there is life in it. Our estimate as to the ability of the preciousness of the seed will have much to do with the result of the seed. If I do not heartily esteem the gospel I teach, I will not teach it with all my heart and cannot expect to see the sheaves. But if I value the gospel, I will share it as being priceless beyond all cost; I will speak with due energy and with an earnestness that brings me to tears. Then I will be the man who comes again rejoicing, bringing my sheaves with me.

He shall doubtless come again. What can this mean except that he will come again to his God? This is what the worker should do after he has labored. If you sought a blessing, go and tell God what you have done, and if you have seen a blessing come, give Him thanks. Those men who went from God with their seed always come back to God with their sheaves. Some workers can see souls converted and take the honor to themselves. But that man who sowed in tears has learned his own weakness in the school of bitterness, and now when he sees results, he comes back again. He comes back to God, for he feels that it is a great wonder that even a single soul should be convinced or converted under such poor words as his.

He shall doubtless come again. Doesn't that mean in the longest and largest sense that He will come again to heaven? He came forth from heaven. His body had not been there, but His soul had; He had communed with God. Heaven was His portion and His heritage, but it was expedient for Him to come here for the sake of others. So in a certain sense, He left the heaven of His rest to go into the field of sorrow among the sons of men. But He shall come again. Ah! Blessed be God, we are not banished by our service. We are kept outside the pearly gates for a little while, but thanks be to God for the honor of being permitted to be absent from our joys for a time. We are not shut out; we are not banished; we shall doubtless come again. Here is your comfort: you go into the mission field and journey to the most remote parts of the earth to serve God, but you shall come again. There is a straight road to heaven from the most remote field of service, and in this you may rejoice.

He shall doubtless come again with rejoicing. What will he rejoice in? When Christian service is done, and Christian reward is rendered, the work endured in serving God, the disappointment, and the racking of heart will make material for everlasting song. Oh, how we will bless God to think that we were counted worthy to do anything for Christ! Was I enlisted in the host that stood the shock of battle? Did the Master allow me to have a hand on the standard that waved amidst the smoke of the battle? Did He allow me to leap into the ditch or scale the rampart? Did He allow me to watch by the baggage while the battle was raging afar off? Then am I thankful that He permitted me to have a share in the glory of that triumphant conflict. Then, as old soldiers show their scars, and as the warriors delight to tell of hairbreadth escapes and of dangers grim and ghastly, so shall we rejoice as we return to God to tell of our going forth and our weeping when we carried the precious seed. Coming back rejoicing, *bringing his sheaves with him.* I do not suppose that the reaper will bring home all his sheaves on his own back, but as an old expositor says, he comes with the cart behind him, with the wagons at his heels, bringing his sheaves with him. Yes, they are *his* sheaves. "How so? All saved souls belong to Christ; they are God's." Yes, but they also belong to the worker. A kind

> Oh, how we will bless God to think that we were counted worthy to do anything for Christ!

of sacred property exists, and God acknowledges men and women who bring souls to Christ.

The true worker will be a reaper. I may sound as though I am speaking to ministers, but I am not. If you are a true worker, you will doubtless be a reaper. Why? First, because the promise of God says so. *So shall my Word be that goes forth out of my mouth: it shall not return unto me void, but it shall accomplish that which I please, and it shall be prospered in that for which I sent it* (Isaiah 55:11). Secondly, God's honor in the gospel requires it. If there is a failure, and you have preached the true gospel, it will be the gospel that fails – but God's attributes are all wrapped up in the gospel, so why would it fail? It is His wisdom and His power. Shall God's wisdom be confused, and God's power be put back? Again, if you persist in sowing, you will reap, because the analogy of nature assures it. The poor peasant, whose little stock of corn is all but spent, takes a little wheat, which is very precious to him, and with many tears he drops it into the soil in the winter months. But God gives him a harvest. In due time, in the mellow autumn days, he gathers in the sheaves, which reward him for his self-denial. It will be so with you. God doesn't mock the farmer; He appoints the seedtime, and He brings around the harvest.

Remember those who have gone before you in this service, who have proved this fact. Think of those you have known who have been successful. They spent their life-power in their Lord's work when their hearts were broken and bruised. Remember Adoniram Judson and the thousands of the Karen people who sing of the Savior whom he first taught to them.[17] Think of Robert Moffat in the kraals of the Bechuanas, not without glorious seals to his ministry. Think of our own missionaries and the multitudes that were turned to Christ during revival seasons in our own land, and you have proof that those who know how to reap and sow and go forth from God shall come again, rejoicing with their sheaves.

---

17   Adoniram Judson (1788-1850) was the first Caucasian American missionary to Burma, where he served for forty years.

About the Author

Charles Haddon (C. H.) Spurgeon (1834-1892) was a British Baptist preacher. He started preaching at age 17, and quickly became famous. He is still known as the "Prince of Preachers," and frequently had more than 10,000 people present to hear him preach at the Metropolitan Tabernacle in London. His sermons were printed in newspapers, translated into many languages, and published in many books.

The Soul Winner
by Charles H. Spurgeon

As an individual, you may ask, *How can I, an average person, do anything to reach the lost?* Or if a pastor, you may be discouraged and feel ineffective with your congregation, much less the world. Or perhaps you don't yet have a heart for the lost. Whatever your excuse, it's time to change. Overcome yourself and learn to make a difference in your church and the world around you. It's time to become an effective soul winner for Christ.

As Christians, our main business is to win souls. But, in Spurgeon's own words, "like shoeing-smiths, we need to know a great many things. Just as the smith *must* know about horses and how to make shoes for them, so we *must* know about souls and how to win them for Christ." Learn about souls, and how to win them, from one of the most acclaimed soul winners of all time.

Available where books are sold.

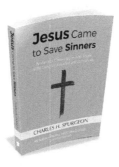

Jesus Came to Save Sinners
by Charles H. Spurgeon

This is a heart-level conversation with you, the reader. Every excuse, reason, and roadblock for not coming to Christ is examined and duly dealt with. If you think you may be too bad, or if perhaps you really are bad and you sin either openly or behind closed doors, you will discover that life in Christ is for you too. You can reject the message of salvation by faith, or you can choose to live a life of sin after professing faith in Christ, but you cannot change the truth as it is, either for yourself or for others. As such, it behooves you and your family to embrace truth, claim it for your own, and be genuinely set free for now and eternity. Come and embrace this free gift of God, and live a victorious life for Him.

Available where books are sold.

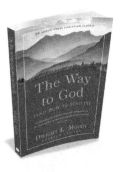

The Way to God
by Dwight L. Moody

There is life in Christ. Rich, joyous, wonderful life. It is true that the Lord disciplines those whom He loves and that we are often tempted by the world and our enemy, the devil. But if we know how to go beyond that temptation to cling to the cross of Jesus Christ and keep our eyes on our Lord, our reward both here on earth and in heaven will be 100 times better than what this world has to offer.

This book is thorough. It brings to life the love of God, examines the state of the unsaved individual's soul, and analyzes what took place on the cross for our sins. The Way to God takes an honest look at our need to repent and follow Jesus, and gives hope for unending, joyous eternity in heaven.

Available where books are sold.

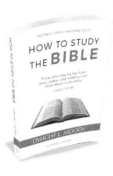

How to Study the Bible
by Dwight L. Moody

There is no situation in life for which you cannot find some word of consolation in Scripture. If you are in affliction, if you are in adversity and trial, there is a promise for you. In joy and sorrow, in health and in sickness, in poverty and in riches, in every condition of life, God has a promise stored up in His Word for you.

This classic book by Dwight L. Moody brings to light the necessity of studying the Scriptures, presents methods which help stimulate excitement for the Scriptures, and offers tools to help you comprehend the difficult passages in the Scriptures. To live a victorious Christian life, you must read and understand what God is saying to you. Moody is a master of using stories to illustrate what he is saying, and you will be both inspired and convicted to pursue truth from the pages of God's Word.

Available where books are sold.